THE AUDACITY
TO DREAM

Stories from an African Immigrant

John Chitakure

John Chitakure

THE AUDACITY TO DREAM
Stories from an African Immigrant

To all underrated and despised immigrants and manual laborers of the world, particularly farm laborers and mafudzan'ombe (cow herders).

John Chitakure

CONTENTS

John Chitakure

PROLOGUE

E veryone has a story to tell. Not an imagined story, but one that flows from one's real-life experiences. A tale that if shared, is capable of entertaining, inspiring, and transforming other people. A narrative that may warm listeners' hearts by reassuring them that every cloud has a silver lining. If humanity had the patience to listen to many of the untold stories, humans wouldn't remain the same. We all have stories to tell. You have your stories, some of which have never been told. I too have real-life stories to share. Yes, they might not be anecdotes of heroic and miraculous deeds, but stories worth listening to. They may not be your kind of stories, but tales that may change your perspective on life.

My stories are a mixed bag—stories of defeats and victories. They are tales of tears and laughter. Accounts of falling and rising again. Stories of my wrestling against inherited poverty. Stories of my struggles to unshackle the seemingly indestructible chains of impecuniosity and exclusion. I write stories of the countless mistakes that I made, and the lessons that I learned from them. Stories in which I met and interacted with people; both good and bad, kind and evil, generous and selfish, poor and rich, sacred and profane, but all were the people that the Creator made. Stories in which some privileged members of the society tried to take away my voice, yet other affluent members of the same community, empowered me.

Life is a journey. There are three types of people that every one of us is likely to meet on our life pilgrimage. You meet people who encourage, assist, respect, and bless you. Those are the people who see some rays of the sun in your struggles when all that you can see is darkness. They advise you not to give up when all that you want to do is to surrender. They push you to do the best you can when all that seems logical for you is to retreat. They point you to new horizons that you never thought existed before when all that you can see isn't further than your own nose. They open new doors of opportunities that you have been blind to. They forgo some of their privileges to make you achieve your personal dreams.

You are also likely to meet people who discourage, demean, and curse you. They convince you that you are good for nothing. They disrespect you. They call you names. They tell you that your options are limited. They persuade you to give up. They try to exploit you. They deny that your opinion matters. They even try to convince other people to treat you like trash. They prevent you from acquiring the things that you deserve. They put barriers between you and your dreams. They criticize every point that you make. They close the doors that others try to open for you. They deny you opportunities that may change your status quo. They do this because they are happy to see you suffer.

The third group of people that you are likely to meet consists of persons who don't care, and might not want to know about you. When they think of human beings, they don't include you. They neither hate nor love you. They are indifferent. They neither demean nor respect you. They neither curse nor bless you. They neither give you a job nor deny you one. You just don't exist. Even if you did, it's none of their business to acknowledge your existence.

I have met all the three groups, and my story involves all of them. If you haven't, you will. I have learned from all of them. Yes, there is so much to be learned from our pain and happiness, tears and laughter, and marginalization and inclusion. It is critical that you take every encounter as a learning opportunity.

They say retelling one's stories is therapeutic, and I believe it. As I was writing these stories, I discovered that putting them on paper was even more healing. There are stories of my life that I have never shared before, and whenever I tried, I would sob. But, now I write them without even shedding a tear. In fact, I have found a new source of inspiration, hope, and strength in narrating them. I relate them not because I have run and finished the race, but because I am still trying. Of course, I have run a good part of the race, and I am determined to persist until I touch the finishing line. I know that it's not over until it's over. I have to begin telling my stories now, for I am not immortal. I don't want to wait until I join the ancestors, hoping that well-wishers would do it for me. Not all of us have the luxury of having someone to tell our tales when we are gone. We do it ourselves, lest we deprive others of valuable lessons.

These stories are real-life narratives extracted from my life experiences. Some of them have never been shared with anyone else. Why do I feel that I should share them now? I share them because they may inspire someone. I tell them because story-telling is therapeutic. I narrate them because old age is creeping on me, and I don't want them to be a burden on my journey to the land of the ancestors. They are stories about the dreams that carried me from the dusty and rocky paths of Nyajena, Masvingo, Zimbabwe, to the now potholed streets of Harare, the capital city of Zimbabwe. Of course, most of them happened before the besieged gods of Zimbabwe had gone crazy. The streets of Harare were still in good shape. Some of the stories occurred at a time when not many Zimbabweans had turned into hunter-gatherers like they have become today. The waterways and drains along the streets of Harare hadn't been neglected, and become filled with debris and nauseating filth.

Mine are stories that saw me rise from the dirty and dusty classrooms of Mudarikwa Secondary School in Masvingo, and landing on the then prestigious and renowned University of Zimbabwe. At that time, it was a great privilege to study at the University of Zimbabwe. I am referring to the era when one was paid for being a student, and that payout was decent enough to pay for one's fees, food, and board, and the change could take one on an unlimited beer drinking kwaMai Fafi or kuLizie (These were famous drinking places for the UZ students). The janitor was still the *sabhuku* (leader) of the foyer, from where he sold life-giving buns to the students who would have squandered all their payout at October Four (a beer hall that was located in the Student Center at the University of Zimbabwe). I write about a time when someone was employed to make up your bed and clean your bedroom. The University of Zimbabwe was still a world-class university, not the shadow of itself that it has become now.

I write about the same dreams that took me from the potholed streets of Harare to the windy city of Chicago, where I experienced snow for the first time. At first, I was so thrilled by the snow, but soon I got tired of it. I also got fed-up of the icy winds of Chicago that dared to freeze my African tears right on my eyelids, as I walked along Madison Street. I got tired of the layers of clothes that I needed to pile onto myself before I dared to step out of the house. But I soldiered on. That's what Zimbabweans do—they brave the winds, a characteristic that has been mistaken for eternal resilience by some Zimbabwean politicians.

Chicago was not unfriendly through and through, for it had its fair share of inspirational places. Whenever I felt overwhelmed by my studies or my constant homesickness, I would just walk to the nearby Lake Michigan to see the frozen waters. The sight of the lake soothed my almost frozen spirits. The waters had some therapeutic touch to my poor soul that had grown tired of snow, studies, and loneliness.

The same dreams brought me here, to the complicated and confusing crossroads of San Antonio, Texas, where almost every driver behaves like a Zimbabwean kombi driver. Those who know a thing or two about Zimbabwe's kombi drivers wouldn't take this as a compliment. Here, in San Antonio, where we eat tacos for breakfast, lunch, and super, and still feel we want some more. Where we have tamales for special days. Where we consume chicken every day, and veggies on special days. I have every reason to believe that the consummation of my life-long dreams lies somewhere here, in this cowboy city. You know why I think so? When we bought our brand-new home in 2014, the ancestors gave me a sign. As I was inspecting the backyard of our newly acquired and cherished property, I came across a plant that looked so familiar—*nyevhe* (Spider flower). Yes, *nyevhe* in America. I meticulously transplanted the sacred seedlings into a well-manured bed, and until now we have plenty of *nyenvhe*. How could we have *nyevhe*, in Texas unless the ancestors planted it for us? But, how could the ancestors have thought of planting *nyevhe* in Texas unless they wanted us to make Texas our new home?

I hope that my story won't only entertain people but also inspire them to transcend their social challenges and fight to improve their lives. My story is worthy-reading because it's unique. It's different from some of the stories that people have read because it's my personal story. My story isn't an epic of heroism and unprecedented accomplishments, but, nonetheless, a unique story worth telling, and from which other people can learn something.

Some great people wait until they die so that other people can write their stories, but, I can't wait for death. Saints postpone sharing their accounts until they are gone, but I don't have the privilege to procrastinate sharing my story until I am gone because I am not a saint. Why telling it now? First, no one except me can tell my story as best as I can. Second, I am not a celebrity or saint, and, no one will ever try to narrate my story when I am gone. Third, telling my story gives me more hope that things will be alright, not only to me but also to others who find themselves in similar situations. Fourth, people can learn and find inspiration not only in stories of somebodies; but also from stories of nobodies like me. Last, I like story-telling, mainly, my own story. Telling it as it is. Saying it the way I want. Narrating it at my own pace. Telling it using my own vocabulary. It gives me energy.

You may not enjoy reading my story, but I still insist that you try it. You may not obtain a significant lesson from it, but I again ask that you read it. My story may not inspire you, and I forgive you for that. I know that you aren't me, but that's not a good reason to ignore it. You know why I insist? So that you get the courage to tell your own story that I think is more inspiring than mine. You don't need to become a politician, celebrity, hero, or saint to be able to tell your story because every story is worth listening to, and learning from.

CHAPTER 1

John Chitakure

KUTAMA COLLEGE AND OTHER SACRED PLACES

The job advertisement was on the front page of the Sunday Mail, which is one of the government-owned weekly newspapers in Zimbabwe. Kutama College wanted an Advanced Level Accounting teacher, with immediate effect. Kutama College was built in 1914 by the Jesuits. It is a Catholic, independent, boarding, high school located near Norton in the Zvimba area about 80 kilometers Southwest of Harare. Kutama has a student population of approximately 900 boys. In Zimbabwe, children spend seven years (from Grade One to Seven) in primary school, after which they qualify for secondary education at high school. They spend at least four years in secondary school, at the end of which they get a General Certificate of Secondary Education (GCSE), which is popularly known as 'O' Level (Ordinary Level). In the past, all the examinations were set and graded in Great Britain, at either Cambridge or London University. Currently, these responsibilities have been surrendered to the Zimbabwe Schools Examinations Council (ZIMSEC), which has its headquarters in Harare. However, students who wish to take the Cambridge University Ordinary or Advanced Level examinations in Zimbabwe can still do so. This certificate, if it comprises at least five subject passes, including the English Language, enables the holder to undergo training at the institutions of tertiary learning.

Nowadays, the 'O' Level subject passes have to include Mathematics and Science. There is an additional two-year period in secondary school, which is referred to as Advanced Level ('A' Level). In the past, 'A' Level was the prerequisite for enrolling at the University of Zimbabwe, which was the only university in the country until 1991 when the National University of Science and Technology (NUST) was established in Bulawayo. In the past, very few schools were qualified to offer Advanced Level classes, so it was a privilege to enroll for it.

Let's go back to Kutama College. I felt that Kutama College had a valid reason for placing that advert on the front page of such a prominent newspaper. Yes, they wouldn't put an advert on the front page of a weekly newspaper unless they had valid and compelling reasons for doing so because it's expensive. It seemed that Kutama College was desperate to get a teacher. They needed to get a commercial subjects teacher as soon as possible. Qualified, Advanced Level Accounting teachers were scarce at that time. It's not that the universities in Zimbabwe were producing less of them, but because their services were also on demand in other sectors of the economy. More so, some Zimbabwean professionals had already started migrating to other countries in search of greener pastures. The economy had started its unprecedented and unstoppable meltdown, and many professionals had begun jumping out of the sinking Titanic of Africa. They had already foreseen the inability of the government to turn around the collapsing economy. In the eyes of optimists and the prophets of hope like me, such pessimists were considered the false prophets of doom.

I later learned that sometimes it pays to be a pessimist. Some of us stayed on, hoping that things would become better, but they didn't. Of course, time proved us wrong—very wrong indeed. The economic situation became irreversibly worse, and we paid heavily for our blind optimism. While others were selling their properties to buy air tickets to go to the West, we were busy applying for jobs in Zimbabwe. While others were leaving Kutama College, we were desperate to find teaching places there. The Kutama teaching position was a perfect fit for my wife. Although my wife had majored in Economics, I knew that she stood a better chance of getting the Kutama job. She had studied accounting at Advanced Level and had taken a course or two in Accounting in her undergraduate studies at UZ. She had the required teaching experience too. At that time, she was teaching Advanced Level Accounting, Management of Business, and Economics at a government high school in Hurungwe.

I didn't waste time. You don't misspend time when you see an opportunity like that. I went to a telephone booth that was outside the UZ Great Hall, perhaps one of the few, which hadn't been vandalized by the UBA or USA (University Bachelors Association, University Spinsters' Association, respectively). Generally, every male student at the University of Zimbabwe was referred to as UBA, and the non-UZ students were the NABA (Non-Academic Bachelors Association), which didn't make any sense. The female students were called USA, and non-UZ female students were NASA) It was at the time when cellphones were beyond the reach of many of us. I will tell you later how I got my first cell phone.

At that time, cell phones were a symbol of civilization, wealth, and success. Very few people owned them. The rest of us had to make use of the remaining public call boxes, which at that time were becoming scarce due to the lack of care by the parastatal that had a monopoly over telecommunications. I was lucky, my phone call got through to Kutama College without a hitch. The call was promptly answered by a female voice. She quickly transferred me to the school head. When the school head responded, he had an incredibly smooth, kind, and fatherly voice. From the way the conversation started, I could sense that it was my lucky day. Yes, it was. My wife was invited for an interview, and she got the job. Yes, she did. Moreover, I was promised a teaching post as soon as I completed my post-graduate studies in education at UZ. That was in 2002. I will give you the details of what transpired in due course.

At the beginning of 2003, I joined Kutama College as a History teacher. I consider my teaching at Kutama College as my last most significant accomplishments as a high school teacher. It was an achievement because being a teacher at Kutama wasn't a mean feat. The school was like a national historic site because former President Robert Mugabe, the only leader Zimbabweans had known since the country's independence from Britain in 1980, was educated there (President Mugabe left office in 2017, November, and was succeeded by Emmerson Mnangagwa). As if that wasn't amazing enough, the school was located in the former President Mugabe's rural village, Kutama, from which it got its name. His iconic thatched house stood about a stone's throw from the college.

This was amazing because it doesn't happen all the time that a man who was educated at Mudarikwa Secondary School, can have the opportunity to inspire the minds of young men at a first-class Catholic high school, run by Marist brothers, and built in the former President's village. Because of the reputation of the school, many government ministers, and other influential and wealthy people scrambled to enroll their children there. Later, the former President's son came to study there, and I was privileged to be his History teacher for a year or two. Yes, one could be lucky to study or teach at Kutama, but to be the first son's teacher was an unexpected opportunity. My enthusiasm about this chance doesn't mean that I was his father's avid supporter. No. I was almost apolitical at that time. Also, I was a teacher, and teachers don't discriminate against any of their students on political grounds.

Like other students in that class, he seemed to enjoy my History lessons. I didn't have to challenge him because he was a good student. Of course, one day I had to reprimand him when I found him sitting on his chair, with his head resting on the desk, and covered with his blazer. I encouraged him to stay awake and reminded him that if his father had behaved in that way during his days at Kutama, he wouldn't have become the President of Zimbabwe. I advised him to remove his blazer from his head to which he politely obliged. I am not sure about what I would have done if he had refused to remove the blazer from his head. Now that it belongs to the past, I don't want to imagine it.

Kutama was a dream school for many students and teachers. The classrooms were big and well-furnished, albeit with old furniture. The students were brighter, politer, and more ambitious, which made it undemanding to facilitate their learning activities. Even the most ungifted teacher would be valuable at Kutama because most students needed less guidance. The headmaster was so kind, caring, and somewhat wise. The teachers' houses were like mansions. Electricity was almost for free. Water was for free. The home backyards were spacious. I mention the backyards because I have a penchant for vegetable gardening. In fact, I ended up planting fruit trees and sugarcane, which still exist at the schoolhouse that I occupied. There were several other incentives for the teachers at Kutama College that educators at other schools didn't have. One of the most popular and envied incentive for Kutama teachers was for recording the students' attendance roster. All those benefits were given in addition to the basic government salaries.

There were more incentives for being the head of a particular school department such as being a hostel master. Of course, being appointed the head of a specific department, or hostel master had its own politics. The headmaster didn't just nominate a teacher to be in-charge of a unit because he was qualified. There had to be some rationale and advantage to the headmaster and the school for every appointment that he made. Later, I came to understand that some of the posts were allocated to appease and reward the headmaster's avid loyalists and friends. Positions were also used to retain teachers who belonged to the critical departments such as the sciences, commercials, and mathematics. Consequently, undependable teachers would be demoted, and their places were taken up by other critically needed and loyal teachers. That is how the soft-spoken headmaster, who one of the teachers, perhaps the most accomplished Accounting teacher to ever teach at Kutama, Mr. Jonathan Sabeta, nicknamed, "Smooth Operator," or S. O, for short. That was the Kutama that I came to in January 2003.

You don't get a teaching post at a school of Kutama's caliber just because you are a qualified teacher. No. Kutama had to have a bigger picture for recruiting you. I know who buttered my bread—my wife. You wouldn't just come to Kutama through your own efforts unless you were a science, commercials, or mathematics teacher. I was a history and religious studies teacher, and the college had more than enough teachers in those areas.

Pote and Magunje Secondary Schools

But, before my wife and I came to Kutama College, we were stationed at Majunje and Pote Secondary Schools, respectively. This is how we both ended up at Kutama College. As I have already alluded to, Kutama wanted a commercial subjects teacher, and my wife could teach all the three required commercial subjects. She had graduated from the UZ with a Bachelor of Science (Honors) in Economics in 2000 and started teaching Accounting, Economics, and Management of Business at Magunje Government School that had just begun offering Advanced Level classes.

The Advanced Level results of her pioneer students at Magunje had proved that she knew the ropes of teaching the commercials and had done the Province proud.

My wife came to Magunje at the time when a particular dubious man was the school headmaster. That man's professional integrity was questionable, at least, according to my own judgment. Although I wouldn't claim to be a perfect judge of character, the manner in which the head of Magunje carried himself left nothing to the imagination. Also, some of his teachers with whom I socialized complained about his unprofessional and erratic behavior. On two different occasions, I had a nasty confrontation with that man.

This is what happened. When my wife graduated from UZ in 2000, I had been teaching at Pote Secondary School for a year. Pote was a remote and rural high school, situated in a Resettlement Area between the cities of Karoi and Chinhoyi. There was no public transport to and from the school. The nearest bus stop was called Bennett, which was situated along the Harare–Chirundu Highway. After alighting from the bus at Bennett, one would finish the remaining twenty kilometers to the school using Adam's mode of transport (feet). The journey wasn't unchallenging, but walkable. The trip was painless for those who owned bicycles like the acting headmaster of Pote Secondary School, Mr. Border Mapani. He had just acquired a brand new Nomax bicycle when I joined his staff. I later purchased my own bike because of necessity, and of course, his encouragement. This significant acquisition made my trips to and from Bennett much enjoyable and more manageable.

At Pote, most students were struggling academically but were well-behaved and well-meaning. Their parents had joyful hopes for their kids just like any other parents elsewhere. Although the villagers were low-income subsistence farmers, they supported both their children and teachers in all possible ways. At first, Pote seemed repulsive to me, but eventually, I discovered that falling in love with it wasn't impossible. When I arrived at the school, I planned to leave as soon as I could, but I ended up staying longer. That is what Pote did to teachers. A newly appointed teacher would vow to quit the school the next day after his arrival, only to stay put for several years.

There were several things about the school that made it repulsive to teachers at first sight. First, the school was situated far away from the nearest bus stop. Second, there were only two classroom blocks that were still under construction. Both had no cement floors. Third, the drinking water was drawn from a borehole, which was almost a mile away from the teachers' residential area. Moreover, the nearest shopping center was about three miles away from the school. As if that wasn't challenging enough, there was no electricity at the school. Additionally, the staff houses were insufficient for the teachers. The seven teachers and their families had to share the three houses that were available at the school.

Like most of the teachers at Pote, I found myself falling in love with the place, and I stayed longer than I had initially planned to. I was still teaching at Pote when my wife completed her degree program at UZ, in August of 2000. When she graduated, we thought that it would be convenient for both of us if she could come over to Pote and temporarily teach at Sungwi, the nearest Primary School that had many big houses for the teachers. At Pote, I had only one room, and if my wife got a place to teach at Sungwi, then I would move over to Sungwi to live there while continuing teaching at Pote. That movement wouldn't only benefit me but would create an extra room at Pote for other teachers who desperately needed additional living space. The headmaster of Sungwi, Mr. Bhasera, was glad that my wife was willing to come and teach at his school. My wife had to start the application process. At some point, the three of us had to go to the District Staffing Offices at Magunje Business Center so that she could fill out the required employment papers. My only role was to take care of our baby, Mufaro, who at this time was about one-year-old. When my wife presented her qualifications to the Education Staffing Officer, he became agitated, but for a good reason.

"Why do you want to waste this intelligent woman's talents, teaching at a primary school? We have been looking for a teacher who has these qualifications to teach our Advanced Level students at Magunje High School. As of now, the students have no teacher. We need you at Magunje, not Sungwi. You are over-qualified for Primary school kids. If you agree to come to Magunje, we will also offer your husband a teaching place at the same school as soon as we have an opening in his area of expertise. We want couples to live and work together because that's the new government policy." He won. My wife went to Magunje High School, and we were happy. Magunje was a good school. There was affordable housing for the teachers, tarred roads, and reliable transportation. There were more than a dozen shops and butcheries. And of course, there were about sixteen beer halls. That was the time when the legendary business mogul, Mr. Kitsiyatota was recovering from his temporary setback.

Like any other faithful men would do, I shuttled to and from Magunje every weekend. I eagerly waited for a teaching post to come up at Magunje, and it surely did, at the end of 2001. This doesn't mean that I wasn't happy at Pote; I was. As a matter of fact, I had been elevated to the position of acting deputy headmaster by the then acting headmaster, Mr. Border Mapani. The post wasn't substantive, but it had its fair share of privileges and benefits. But, naturally, I wanted to be with my family at Magunje. Pote and Magunje were in the same education District. Thus, the transference process would be less tedious and faster.

The Job Interview and the Unethical School Head

Magunje Secondary School wanted a Divinity teacher. Everything within me told me that the post was ear-marked for me, for Divinity was my undisputed area of specialization. I had studied the New Testament under Dr. Ainos Moyo; a brilliant biblical scholar. I had also learned New Testament Greek, which gave me an added advantage over those candidates who hadn't studied the ancient language. In addition to that, I had taken advanced Old Testament studies under the Rev. Dr. Philimon Chikafu. Those who know these two professors would agree with me that they were among the best in the Religious Studies, Philosophy, and Classics Department at UZ during our time. I was also confident that I would get the job because I had an ace in the pack—my wife. They needed her services in the commercial subjects department, and there was no way they would refuse to offer me the job. I was wrong. I was very wrong, indeed, for the school head lacked that conventional wisdom. I didn't get the job. I attended the interview, and I performed exceedingly well as far as I could judge. It was a panel interview, and they made a mistake of asking me content questions. I was still fresh from college, and I had the required data oozing out of my fingertips. Undoubtedly, I immensely impressed the panelists, but then something strange happened. The headmaster who had been quiet up to that point started shouting at me. Yes, he was distraught with me.

"Mr. Chitakure, why do you want to impose yourself on this school?" That was his first irrelevant and unprofessional question. I was completely flabbergasted. The panelists were petrified too. Before I could recover from the effects of that question, the school head gave me some more. "Why are you so desperate to get a job at this school? For your own information, I am the head of this school, and I reserve the right to employ the teacher of my choice. I don't care about the impression that you may have made to these teachers. I am in charge." He paused, looked at me directly in the eyes, and attempted a smile. His contemptuous grin drew my attention to his Hitler-like mustache. He was devilish. There was no doubt about that. He seemed to be enjoying the circus too. I still don't understand why he felt that I was trying to impose myself on his school. This was a job interview, and I only answered the questions that were asked as truthfully as I could.

I think that he didn't expect me to be all that good. He had hoped that my performance would be sub-standard, and that would justify him not offering me the post. Furthermore, the excitement and contentment my answers generated among the panelists might have added gas to fire. He became aware that they were going to recommend me for the job, and that would leave him with little room to refuse. He decided to stop the interview by making personal attacks on me. As he continued to waffle, I knew that my dream of coming to Magunje High School to join my family was shuttered. I remained quiet. But, I had to recover quicker than others because it was my future at stake here.

"With all due respect, Sir, I don't understand what you are talking about. Would you please, elaborate what you have just said?" I tried harder to keep my cool.

"I don't repeat myself. You have heard me," thundered the bull of Magunje High School. He was the school head, and his word was final. The panelists were just there to assist him and make some recommendations that he could take or reject.

"Sir, I don't think that I am imposing myself unto this school. You advertised a teaching vacancy in my area of expertise, in a public newspaper. I applied. You invited me to this interview. I came. You ask me questions, and I answer them to the best of my ability. I really don't understand why that can be interpreted as an imposition. I consider it my constitutional right, as a citizen of Zimbabwe, to be able to apply for any job for which I am qualified without the fear of being accused of trying to impose myself."

I had just come out of UZ, and student politics were still raw in my head. I didn't think that student politics wouldn't save me here. Of course, student politics had proved to be sterile even during our time at UZ. In 1999, the students had failed to prevent UZ from being privatized, despite the likes of Learnmore Jongwe, Job Wiwa Sikhala, Jethro Mpofu (Bolekaje), and other talented student leaders' impressive and insightful harangues directed to Dr. Ignacious Chombo, the then Minister of Tertiary and Higher Education, not to. Nobody listened to them. Sometimes political leaders prefer to listen to their voice of power than that of wisdom. Students had the wisdom, but the politicians had the power, and the power won. Consequently, UZ was privatized, and that marked the beginning of the UZ students' tribulations. It brought about the pauperization of the students at UZ, and eventually, at other Zimbabwean universities.

In that room, I knew that the head of Magunje had already decided my fate, and there was nothing that I could say that would make him change his mind. Everyone was quiet. They were afraid of him. There are times when you are conscious of the futility of your own words and arguments, but you still argue. I continued. "Second, I am qualified for the job. I am probably the best teacher you can ever get to teach Divinity. The panelists may testify to that." Nobody did. "Third, my wife teaches here, and it was made abundantly clear by the District Education Staffing Officer, in your presence that I would be considered for a vacancy in Divinity at this school whenever it arises. We all know that's the new government directive that Mr. Aenaeas Chigwedere, the Minister of Education, Sports, and Culture has promulgated." The panelists were impressed, but the headmaster wasn't. He looked angrier. I can't remember the details of how the interview ended, but I was sure that he wasn't going to give me the job. I left the interview room unceremoniously. There were no pleasantries exchanged. The whole episode reminded me of how vulnerable to the unfair treatments I was as a job seeker.

What the unscrupulous school head did next was unexpected and selfish. He froze the post because the panelists had recommended me as the best candidate for the position despite his dishonorable rantings. He couldn't successfully contest that because each one of the panelists had a score sheet that the headmaster couldn't alter. Moreover, the score sheets could possibly be presented to higher officers as a report of what transpired during the interview. If need be, the same could provide evidence of my academic and professional acumen to the powers that be. So, he froze the post. Yes, he had the authority to do that. He deprived the unsuspecting and innocent students of Magunje of a teacher because he didn't like me. That is what arrogance and corruption do if perpetrated by those who wield unchecked power. They make third parties suffer unnecessarily.

You can imagine how I felt about that unfairness, injustice, and contempt of professionalism by a senior government official. What I did next, I wouldn't do now, if the incident were to repeat itself. When you are young, and fresh from college, you erroneously think that you can change the world. You believe that some people at the top of the system still have a conscience, and can assist you to achieve justice. Now, having been an ardent student of experience, I know better. I understand that idealism is different from realism. I realize that some evil and unjust systems can't be transformed overnight.

I went to the District Education Office at Magunje to lodge a formal complaint about the unethical behavior of the headmaster of Magunje. The officers there did nothing to appease my humiliated and marginalized soul. In fact, the senior Education Officers seemed to be afraid of the headmaster. I still don't know why. They were his superiors and understood that his behavior at the interview was unprofessional, yet they were reluctant to reprimand him. I tried to remind them of the promise that they had made to me when they employed my wife, and to my greatest disappointment, they didn't seem to remember it. I then decided to escalate the issue to the Provincial Education Offices in Chinhoyi. What a waste of time and energy!

When I arrived there, I demanded to see the Regional Director of Education, who at the time was a wonderful lady, but her secretary wouldn't allow me to meet her. I had to schedule an appointment for a meeting with her, just like all other disgruntled civil servants would. That was the protocol. But, I was fresh from college, where nobody followed protocol. As students at the University of Zimbabwe, we could just march along Second Street, and gather at Minister Chombo's Old Mutual offices without warning. I wasn't going to follow protocol now.

I threatened to stay in until I could see her, and her secretary relented. She was summoned, and I narrated to her what had happened, and how frustrated I was. "Thank you, Madam, for sparing some time to hear my case. I am aware of your busy schedule, and I appreciate your understanding. I come to you not only as the Provincial Director of Education but also as a mother." I got her attention, and I narrated my story. She consoled me and promised to do something about it, but to my knowledge, she didn't do anything about it. I never received any further communication from her as I had expected. I didn't get the job. I didn't get my superiors' intervention as well. The headmaster's arrogance and corruption were vindicated, for he remained the undisputed lion of Magunje High School. He was cruel and unprofessional, but powerful and untouchable. The grapevine had it that he went around telling people that if I wanted to stay with my family, I was supposed to ask the District Staffing Officer to transfer my wife to Pote, where I was teaching. He knew I wouldn't do that. Pote wasn't a place for married couples and families, who could be elsewhere.

So, I was the loser. The headmaster was above the law of justice. He was accountable to no one. I was disappointed. Have you ever felt that you were entitled to something, and then some influential people wouldn't let you have it? Have you ever felt really short-changed and there was nothing you could do about it? Have you ever felt powerless? I mean really impotent. That's how I felt. Have you ever appealed to God because no earthly power could help you? That's what I did, but God didn't answer my prayers. In fact, he seemed oblivious to my plight? I never realized that God works according to God's time, not human time. I learned that if you expect God to meet deadlines based on human time, you would, most of the time, find him wanting. Just allow God to do the things that God does at God's own pace and time, and you will never run short of miracles.

The Magunje abuse inflicted deep wounds on me, but I healed. Sometimes, time performs miracles on our wounded hearts. The incident also taught me the lesson that injustice can be difficult to eradicate. My wife and I gracefully accepted our powerlessness and its consequences. But, God and the ancestors intervened. It is true that when all doors seem to have closed on you, somewhere, God opens a window. The only challenge is that most people concentrate on force-opening the closed doors instead of looking for the opened window. Those who waste their time begging the closed doors to open will continue to languish in their despair because they may fail to see the rays of light that come through the hidden opened window.

Saint Eric's High School and Kutama College

It was at that point that Kutama College advertised for a commercials teacher. My wife got the job. As if that was not good enough, the headmaster also invited me to teach at Kutama, after completing my one-year Graduate Certificate in Education studies that I had barely started at the University of Zimbabwe. Yes, my wife got the job, but that wasn't the end of the story. The unethical headmaster of Magunje was mortified. He refused to clear my wife, not only because he was a sadist, but because he knew how difficult it would be for him to find another commercial subjects teacher of my wife's caliber. I also think that he was jealous because Kutama College wasn't only the best school in Mashonaland West Province but also a force to reckon with, nationally. My wife went to the District Education Offices, where the Staffing Officer cleared her from Karoi District. She went to Kutama where she started teaching without the headmaster of Magunje's clearance. Since the District office had endorsed her transfer to Kutama, the headmaster's clearance letter wasn't entirely necessary. At long last, justice had been served. I learned that sometimes the powerless, vulnerable, and abused people who surrender their tribulations to supernatural higher powers and wait patiently, do get their prayers answered. Mine was.

Our coming to Kutama College made my commute from Norton's Saint Eric's High School, where I was doing teaching practice, more effortless. Saint Eric's was some other story. The school administration assigned me to teach two classes. I taught History to one level, and Religious Studies to another. I did enjoy teaching the History class more, for the students were younger and eager to learn. What bothered me at Saint Eric's was the Religious Studies class, which comprised students that had failed to make it to the top five streams. Most of the students in that class didn't quite enjoy learning, to say the least. It was in winter, and some students would refuse to enter the classroom, just preferring to sit along the outside walls of the school, basking in the sunshine. Occasionally, the deputy headmaster and senior teacher had to persuade them, or compel them to get into the classroom in which lessons were in progress. Despite those noble efforts, some students would still refuse to enter the learning space. As I started teaching, some of the truant students would whip those in the classroom with long sticks, through the open windows. They just wanted to cause a commotion among those who were willing to learn. They wanted the compliant students to stop learning to prevent them from benefitting in their voluntary absence.

Those readers who aren't privy to the Anglo-Zimbabwean education system might not find anything amiss in the behavior of the students in question. Zimbabwean students are expected to love schooling and to do everything in their power to go to school and attend classes. They might be less gifted academically, but they still work hard and hope to improve. It's imperative that they do their homework, and respect the teachers at all times. From time to time, some educational misfits appear, but the school administration deals with them successfully. Most students who study diligently pass their examinations. For me, the behavior of these students wasn't only unacceptable, but it was also unprecedented. I could have disciplined them if had the authority to do so, but I didn't. I was a student teacher and had no power to punish them.

One day, as I was about to administer an end of term examination, one of the students stole the envelop that contained the question papers and hid it. That happened in a fraction of a second. I just placed the packet on the desk and looked to the other side and by the time I checked the table, the papers were gone. I asked them where the package had gone, and no one answered me. Some looked down, and others just gazed at me and giggled. I didn't panic. When you deal with students of that caliber, you shouldn't show any sign of nervousness. If you display any sign of anxiety, they laugh at you.

I went ahead and distributed the answer sheets to all the students. When every student had an answer sheet on the desk and a pen in hand, I told them to start answering the test questions. I knew that they didn't have the question papers. Of course, one of them had the question papers, and the whole class knew who that student was. I started counting down the examination time. It worked. After about ten minutes into the test, I deliberately walked to the door giving them my back, and when I turned back, the question paper package had been placed on the table where I had put it when I entered the classroom. I opened it and distributed the papers, but the countdown continued. I never insisted on finding out who the culprit was because I knew that would be like chasing a wild goose. Students in that class protected each other. Later, when I went to teach at Kutama, I got to know that the students' protection of each other was called *broederbond*, which is the Afrikaner word for brotherhood.

At some point during that term, my University of Zimbabwe tutor came to the school to observe me in action. This observation was one of the requirements for a successful completion of the teaching practice component of the program. We walked to the classroom where the lesson observation was supposed to take place, and to my worst horror, there were no students. Later, I learned that they had run away from school chasing after the Nyau Dancers along the street. Those people who have been student teachers would know that it's tremendously stressful to be observed by a higher officer while teaching. Failure to locate my students was devastating and almost paralyzing.

"Where are your students?" asked the overzealous tutor.

"I don't know. They were here about an hour ago," I responded. I was embarrassed. I had to recover from the shock as soon as I could. One of the senior teachers came to my aid by allowing me to teach his class in the place of my truant one. I had never taught those students before, but it worked. I passed my teaching practice observation. In fact, those students begged me if I could become their permanent teacher. They were sad when I told them that I would be teaching at Saint Eric's for only four months.

That was the spirit of one of my classes at Saint Eric's. Of course, not all the students in that class were mischievous. Many good students at that school were disciplined, intelligent, and respectful. It just happened that I got one of the worst classes. Some of the Saint Eric's students proceeded to university and graduated with flying colors.

An Unpleasant Visit to Magunje Secondary School

For about three months, the headmaster of Magunje kept pestering, threatening, and haunting the headmaster of Kutama, accusing him of having stolen an uncleared teacher from his school. I think that the headmaster of Kutama knew how stubborn and headstrong the Magunje headmaster was, and wanted the issue resolved amicably. One day, the headmaster of Kutama called me and encouraged me to escort my wife to Magunje so that the matter of clearance would be concluded once and for all. That's what happens in life. Some people refuse to assist you when you are in need, and when God answers your prayers, they become jealous. The headmaster of Magunje was disgruntled. He had denied me the opportunity to teach at Magunje, and God had answered our prayers by bringing us to Kutama. He didn't like it. He was a sadist who wanted to see people suffering.

My wife and I went to Magunje and found the headmaster in his office. As I expected, he was angry to see me. I guess he had expected my wife to come alone so that he could ill-treat her without anyone to defend her. Such sadists prey on vulnerable people. I wasn't going to let that happen to my wife. As soon as we entered his imperial office, I greeted him and asked if there was anything that he would need from me, or I would walk out of his office and visit my friends. At that point, he cursed me. I sort of expected it. I could have fought him, but I didn't because of three reasons. First, I don't settle disputes through fighting. My last fight had been in 1983 when I was in Grade Four, and I wasn't going to fight this time.

The 1983 fight was preventable if I had the wisdom that I possess now. Two of my classmates bullied me and took my pen by force. After hours of pleading with them to give back my pen to no avail, I decided to retaliate. I snatched one of their pens, and I refused to give it back until they returned my pen. They didn't. After school as I walked home with my friends, the two little bullies followed me. About half a mile away from the school, they cornered me despite my efforts to evade them. One of them took away all my school books, and the other one started beating me as I tried to escape. Then it suddenly occurred to me that I had to defend myself. In those days, in situations like that one had two options—either to run away or fight. I had tried to run away, and they had outrun me. I remained with only one option; to fight back. I did with unusual vivacity.

I had been involved in numerous pet childhood fights before, but that one was the mother of all. I don't remember my opponent's punches ever landing on me because I was too anxious to notice. I know that I managed to block most of his punches, but a few got me. He hit me, and I hit him back, harder. I punched every part of his body on which I could land my fist. Within a few minutes, his face was bloody, but he kept coming. My friends cheered and jeered, and I continued throwing my punches. My knuckles were sore, but I had to keep him at bay. I can't remember how the fight ended, but it sure did, and I was relieved. Fighting is like a soccer game, if you are leading, you want that game to end as fast as possible because you don't want your opponent to turn the tables on you. The next day, I got to know that he had sustained a cut above his eye. If it had been his eye, I could have been put to task about it although I was defending myself. The thought that someone might have lost his sight in a fight with me has always haunted me. I said to myself, never again. So, I wasn't going to fight the cantankerous headmaster.

Second, the headmaster wasn't an old man, and it was hard to guess his fighting capabilities. I didn't want to start a fight that I wouldn't win. A defeat would cause unbearable humiliation in the presence of my wife. Third, having studied logic, I erroneously thought that every disagreement could be resolved by reasoning. After all, we were both professionals who were expected to value the importance of peaceful conflict resolutions. I was wrong. The more I tried to reason with him, the more irrational and pugnacious he became. He looked like he was possessed by some demons. At that juncture, I had to do what a man has got to do. I must admit that I took off my jacket as if preparing for a bloody boxing contest. Instead of lashing at him in a *Karateka* swipe, I pushed the desk, behind which he was sitting, and its edge pinned him to the wall. At this point, he realized that he could no longer continue to abuse me. I saw fear in his eyes. When he spoke, I could tell that the move had brought him back to his senses. Of course, my wife pacified me before the situation deteriorated into a physical contest. The headmaster agreed to complete the clearance papers. He signed them, and then told us that they had to be stamped. He looked for the school stamp in his drawers but seemed not to find it.

"Oh, I know where it is. I had forgotten that the deputy headmaster borrowed it yesterday, and didn't return it," said the headmaster. He sounded friendly enough to earn our trust. He took the clearance forms and went out promising to come back shortly. I didn't say a thing, and soon I realized my mistake. He didn't come back. He suddenly closed the door behind him and locked it from outside. He cursed and shouted. He then started making frantic phone calls to the police station. He told them that I was beating him up and pleaded with them to come as fast as they could. He wasn't only arrogant, abusive, and unprofessional, but also an unrepentant liar. I hadn't laid a finger on him, and I wasn't going to.

It seemed that the devil was winning again. So, I was going to be arrested. I had never been incarcerated before, and I dreaded the thought of spending a couple of days in police cells. Yes, evil people have a way of winning, most of the time. Many times, I feel that the prophet Jeremiah was justified to ask God why the evil people seemed to prosper all the time. It seems that good people almost always suffer. So, we were illegally detained in the headmaster's office. We sat in that locked room waiting for the arrival of police officers to seal our defeat and humiliation. Sometimes the best you can do is just wait and pray.

I am sorry; I almost forgot to tell you that before this encounter with the law enforcement agents, I had been handcuffed once. It happened at Sam Levy's Village, in Harare, in 1995. Sam Levi's Village is a shopping mall that was built by Sam Levy, a Zimbabwean businessman and property developer in 1990 to cater for the shopping needs of the residents of the flamboyant, low residential area of Borrowdale. When it was opened in 1990, most of the shoppers who frequented it were Whites. It was on Sunday, and I decided to go window shopping at Sam Levy's Village. At that time, I was studying at Wadzanai Training Center, which was about a mile and a half from the village. As I was about to get into the enclosure of the village, coming from the direction where TM Supermarket was located, I was stopped by a police officer.

"I want to see your Identity Card (ID)," the officer demanded. I handed him a college (UZ) Identity Card (ID). He looked at me and laughed. "What's this? This isn't an ID. I want to see your national Identity Card." He meant business.

"I forgot it at the college. May I go back and get it for you? I need about twenty minutes."

"No. Join those people sitting down over there. You are under arrest for failure to produce an official ID when required to do so by a lawful officer," he explained to me. I was shocked because I had never been asked for my ID by a law enforcement agent before that day. As I sat down among a dozen black women and men in the same predicament, I began to observe something sinister. The police officers never stopped white people who were passing through the checkpoint. (The officer was black. In fact, we didn't have white police officers at that time). When I was arrested by the police officer, the white lady in front of me wasn't asked for her ID. More white people came and passed the checkpoint without being asked a thing. I stood up and went to the officer who had arrested me and asked why he wasn't stopping White people. I can't remember the reason he gave me, but he was so unsettled by my question. He ordered me to sit down. After about twenty minutes, we were frog-marched to the back of the Village where a police van was waiting for us. As I was pushed into the stationary car, I was horrified to see one of my college friends, Jacob Madzivire, in handcuffs, sitting in the police van.

"Why is he in handcuffs? You can't tell me that you handcuffed him for not having his ID on him. That's very unfair. Please, uncuff him because he isn't a criminal. He won't run away. Why do you treat people like this?" I was upset.

"What did you just say? Who are you to tell us how to do our job? Do you know that I can lock you up for two days for resisting arrest? You think that being a student at UZ is special?" He knew it was. "I will show you that I am in charge here." He asked me to extend my hands for the cuffs. That was my first time to be cuffed. We were taken to Borrowdale Police Station where we found our college mate, Andrew Matsure, waiting for us with the money to pay our fines. We were released on the same day. Of course, it was later discovered that the Zimbabwean constitution didn't authorize the police to arrest people for not having their national IDs on their persons. This judgment nullified all the past arrests, but no refunds were given to the victims. The legal challenge came as a relief to the poor people of Zimbabwe who were often victimized by the police for failing to produce their IDs on demand. Sometimes it boggles my mind as to how the constitution of a country can be violated for many years without anyone noticing. Now, you can walk around in Zimbabwe without the fear of being arrested for having no official identity papers on your person.

Now let's go back to the Magunje episode. The police officer arrived within fifteen minutes. The headmaster unlocked the door of his pseudo prison, and to my most enormous relief, the officer who attended to us was Constable Bhedhu (not his real name). I knew him from my socializing at Magunje Growth Point. Although we weren't friends, we had exchanged greetings on numerous occasions. He was also shocked to see my wife and me sitting in the self-styled detention center of the headmaster. We could have lodged a complaint about our unlawful detention, but we never thought about it, for we were still in shock. Anyway, to cut a long story short, when the headmaster felt that the officer believed our side of the story and that the law wasn't on his side, he panicked. He started shouting and cursing, but it worsened the situation. The officer was intelligent enough to know that we had done nothing that warranted his actions.

The police officer asked, "Sir, is there any reason why you shouldn't clear Mrs. Chitakure?

"She abandoned her students?" The headmaster answered.

"Is there any law that doesn't allow teachers to transfer to other schools? You just told me that she was cleared by the District Education Officer, what's wrong with that? I don't expect a professional like you to act like that. It's really embarrassing. If she owes the school any money, then tell us so that she pays it back. You don't treat people like this. Do you know that they may press charges against you for unlawful detention? Why are you so cruel?"

When the school head sensed that I had no case to answer, he cried at the top of his voice. It was such a weird cry, the type that penetrates the bone marrow of those who hear it. Again, God had vindicated the down-trodden. The look on his face showed that he wasn't used to being defeated. I pitied him. After admitting that my wife owed the school nothing that prevented him from clearing her, he agreed to sign the clearance letter the following day. But when we went to his office to collect the clearance documents as he had promised on the previous day, we were instructed to meet him at the District Education Offices, which were about a mile from the school. When we got there, he was already sitting and talking to his superiors. The moment he saw me, he started threatening and cursing as he had done the previous day.

We later, learned that he had falsely reported that I had assaulted him. He had lied again. You know what? It's easier to forgive school kids when they blatantly lie to the teacher. But, I don't understand how a powerful, lying headmaster could avoid being judged. I boiled with anger, but I couldn't lay a finger on him. The District Education officers were present, and I couldn't disrespect them. They too seemed to be afraid of the headmaster. Eventually, the headmaster signed the clearance documents and off we went to Kutama. He kept his Magunje, and God led us to Kutama, a far much better school than Magunje High School. He had closed just a small window, and God had opened a door for us.

After that incidence in 2002, I met that headmaster once. He, some of his teachers, and Magunje soccer team had come to Kutama for a Provincial soccer tournament. I went up to where he was standing and greeted him. I invited him and his teachers to come over to my house for a meal, and he flatly declined. Of course, I hadn't expected him to accept the invitation, but I just wanted to show him that I had already moved from the past because I didn't want to be its slave. As a matter of fact, I had no valid reason not to forgive him because his cruelty had forced us to look for other options, and we ended up at Kutama College. If he had given me a teaching post at Magunje High School, my wife wouldn't have thought of applying for a teaching post at Kutama. His cruelty had pushed us to Kutama, and he was supposed to earn credit for that.

As you may all realize, this is my side of the story. It might be interesting to hear the headmaster's side of the same story. Although I have told this story as truthfully as I remember it, the headmaster holds the key to the understanding of why he chose to treat us in the manner that he did. I also omitted some of his nasty insults to my wife and me, since he isn't here to defend himself. I think that by now life has educated him enough to be human. Yes, time transforms everything, at times.

Kutama College, Here I Come

After I completed my Graduate Certificate in Education studies, I immediately joined my wife at Kutama. What an achievement! As I have already said, everything at Kutama was better. The students were more respectful, ambitious, and smarter. The school head was courteous, polite, and understanding. This doesn't mean that he wasn't political, calculating, and somewhat cunning like most administrators are. The first thing that startled me at Kutama was my schedule of classes. When I was interviewed for the post, I had stated, in no uncertain terms that I wasn't ready to offer World and African History up to Advanced Level. I had told them that I would be happier to teach juniors and Ordinary Level students. I had reasons for that request. At UZ, I had studied Religious Studies and Christian History, not secular history. The administrators of Kutama College initially granted my request. However, when schools opened things changed. The senior master told me that I was going to teach history up to Advanced Level. I tried to contest it, but I was told either to shape up or ship out. I reluctantly opted for the former, and I am glad that I did.

Although the senior master sounded cruel, he empathized with me and rendered me the professional support that I needed. He loaned me all his history resource books. As soon as I began to read about the French Revolution, I fell in love with it. I discovered that secular history was laced with church history. Moreover, I had the teaching methodology, and what I only needed was the data. Teaching Advanced Level History enabled me to meet my first group of students. They were very refined and purposeful young men. They were brilliant and vibrant. They were Simba Manyureni, Alex Katsamba, Kesiwe Malindi, Kevin Mudzingwa, Russell. Later, we were joined by one more student whose name I withhold for reasons I shall share later. He is the one that impressed me most, and I will tell you the reason shortly.

At about the same time, the new deputy headmaster of Kutama, Br. Charles (not his real name), had introduced incentives for teachers whose students would have excelled in national examinations. Many teachers who were teaching examination classes, including my wife, had already received the incentives for their best results. I, like most other teachers, aimed at getting the incentives for academic excellence the next year. One day, at the end of my first year at Kutama, I entered the Lower Six classroom to deliver a lecture, and I was disappointed to see a new student sitting at the back of the room. I had taught and prepared my students for a year, and to have a new student joining the class at that time was the surest way of not getting the reward for excellence. Furthermore, it was likely to disturb the flow of the learning process of my other students with whom I had academically connected. I greeted the new student and continued with my teaching as if nothing had happened. But after the lecture, I went to the senior teacher to protest. He listened to my rantings without saying a thing, and then reminded me that it was the prerogative of the administration to enroll students, and my only responsibility was to teach them. He was right, and I was wrong. I accepted the defeat, but begrudgingly.

As you know that water flows downhill, I decided to vent my resentment on the new student. I just ignored him. I pretended that he didn't exist in that class. I was conscious that such behavior was unprofessional, but I felt that it was the only way I could register my disapproval to the school administration. I ignored the fact that the newcomer wasn't part of the administrative staff. That's what frustration does. It blinds and prevents you from perceiving the injustice that you perpetrate on other people. I avoided him. I never asked him a question. When he volunteered with an answer, I never commented. But he wasn't stupid, as I later learned. After a couple of weeks, he got the message. On a Friday morning, as I was leaving the classroom, he followed me and challenged me. "Sir, may I talk to you for a moment?"

"What would you like to discuss with me?" I responded as I stopped to face him.

"Sir, I might be wrong, but I have a feeling that you don't like me. It's not your fault but mine. I know that you have higher expectations for your students. I understand that you are passionate about your teaching, and your standards are high. I am sorry that I joined your class very late. I will need some more time to catch up with the rest of the class. I would like you to know that I studied History before. I wrote the examination and failed. Do you know how it feels to fail an exam?" He paused. I didn't answer because I didn't know how it felt. I had never failed an examination all my academic life.

He continued, "When I was told that I was coming to Kutama, I was excited. I knew that this time I would make it. My first day in your class proved me right. There is no way I can fail the History examination with a teacher like you. Please, assist me. I can do extra work to catch up with other students." I was both perplexed and impressed. I had never been challenged by a student like that before. If I were in his shoes, I wouldn't have gathered the courage similar to his. The student knew what he wanted and how to achieve it. He was smart. Indeed, I was disarmed. I looked at him admiringly and promised that I would do everything within my professional capacity to help him pass the History examination. I meant it. When the Advanced Level examinations results came out the following year, he had an "A" in History. I still celebrate the lesson that he taught me. He taught me to be compassionate and empathetic. He taught me to think of my students' success first before I can think of my personal benefits and comfort. He taught me not to think of myself all the time, but to think of the needs of others. His words still move me whenever I retell the story.

The Politics of Kutama College

Although Kutama College was like pure heaven for somebody like me who had taught and lived at Pote Secondary School, it had its politics and challenges. One of the difficulties concerned the use of the school phone that was situated in the staffroom. This is what transpired. It was at the time when very few teachers had cell phones because they were beyond their reach. Most teachers at Kutama had to rely on the school landline that would bring calls through the headmaster's secretary, who would then transfer them to the staffroom extension phone. The extension phone wasn't programmed to make out-going calls. For some of us who couldn't afford a cell phone, this arrangement was a big blessing. Then, one day, the extension landline to the staffroom was gone. Just like that. It wasn't stolen but removed. We reported for work on a Wednesday morning, and the handset was gone. We later learned that it had been removed by the college administrators. There was no logical reason given for removing it except that some teachers attended classes late while answering calls. So, it was deemed necessary to remove the phone.

People still tried to get in touch with the teachers through the school landline, and the secretary would take down the messages and pass them on to the teachers. Like some of us, she sometimes forgot to convey the received communication. She forgot to relay the news about my cousin's death. This is what transpired. My cousin died in Chivi, and my brother called and left a message with the school secretary. She forgot to pass the sad news to me. She only remembered to do that a couple of days later. Even then, she gave the message to my sister-in-law, who also forgot to convey it to me for a day or two. When I finally got the news, the funeral had already taken place, and I had missed it. I was devastated.

My cousin, Sostinah, was important to me for many reasons. She visited us in 1989 when I was in Form Three at Mudarikwa Secondary School. It was in winter. I didn't have a warm jersey or jacket to wear to school during those winter mornings. She felt pity for me and donated her own jersey to me. She, being smaller than I was, the jersey's sleeves were shorter than my arms, but it served the purpose. I used it until I finished my Ordinary Level studies. She had contributed to who I had become, yet I missed her funeral. I was agitated. If the staffroom extension line hadn't been removed, I wouldn't have missed the funeral. I was angry with the person who had disconnected the extension phone from the staffroom. Someone had worked hard to bring that handset into the staffroom, and another person was so unthoughtful as to reverse that valuable incentive. I had a solution. My wife and I borrowed some money from a friend. We bought a cell phone line. The same friend loaned us his handset, and we were good to go. That's how we got our first cell phone.

The following day after we acquired our precious and indispensable gadget, I hit the cup. As per tradition, any teacher who wanted to announce something to the staff would attract their attention by beating the edge of an empty teacup with a spoon. That would happen at the ten o'clock tea break when most teachers gathered for tea. The effects of such a sound were magnetic. Everyone would stop talking and eating to give undivided attention to the person hitting the cup. There was no protocol about tea break annunciations. Any teacher could just hit the cup to draw attention, and everybody would listen. I did.

"Good morning everyone, I have an announcement to make. I now have a cell phone." I lifted it up for everyone to see. "I would like to thank the administration for removing the landline extension from the staffroom. It made me think. Now, with this cell phone, I won't miss any funeral of a relative like I did last time. I will take it into every classroom in which I teach, and I will answer it whenever it rings. It's different from the extension phone that couldn't be carried to the classrooms. To other teachers, I say. Open your eyes. Make some sacrifices. Buy your own cell phones." Of course, I wasn't going to answer the phone during lessons. Some teachers clapped hands for me, and others didn't, mainly the administrators and their surrogates. Within a couple of weeks, some teachers followed suit. They bought their own cell phones.

One other setback that happened at Kutama was the garnishment of my incentive by the acting headmaster because of the false report about me that one of the sports administrators, a fellow teacher, had presented to him. We had had a swimming gala for our students. All the teachers were assigned to respective student houses as animators. During the competitions, I had participated actively, cheering the competitors who belonged to my house. This celebration took place on a Saturday. Monday morning came, and it was the day when we were supposed to receive our monetary incentives. I was shocked because I got nothing. When I enquired why I hadn't received anything, I was then told that my benefits had been garnished because I hadn't participated actively during the gala.

It was a blatant lie. But, the decision couldn't be reversed. It was one of the unfairest things to happen to me at Kutama because the monetary incentive wasn't only for sporting activities. It was also for other roles such as recording the attendance roster, and for being the departmental head. But all the incentive money was withheld. Even if the sports administrator felt justified to penalize me for not committing myself entirely during the Saturday gala, I felt that only a proportionate amount was supposed to be subtracted from my incentive, not everything. No one listened to my argument. They took everything. After petitioning higher officers about the grievance to no avail, I ignored the setback. I wasn't a novice to being mistreated, and I wasn't going to cry over it now.

Another big challenge that I encountered at Kutama happened in 2005 after my wife had transferred from the Ministry of Education to join the Ministry of Finance in Harare. At almost the same time, the school deputy headmaster, who had acted as the school head for nearly a year was demoted. The demoted school deputy head started persecuting and harassing teachers, particularly Catholics. At first, I was spared the harassment. There was a time when several school headmasters were suspended by the then Minister of Education, Sport, and Culture, Mr. Aeneas Chigwedere because they had raised school fees without the Ministry of Education's approval. During that time, the deputy headmaster of the school had taken over as the acting headmaster. He was a very productive and pragmatic leader, and I respected him for that.

When the headmaster was eventually reinstated, there came some tension at the school. This strain was worsened by the demotion of the deputy headmaster and his replacement by another religious brother. The demoted deputy refused to vacate his office. To avoid direct confrontation with him, the headmaster and his new deputy converted the almost dilapidated Geography room into a new office for the new deputy. That didn't go well with Brother Charles, who started harassing teachers and writing warning letters to several of them. As I mentioned above, I wasn't targeted initially, but one day all hell broke loose. I was summoned to his office and received a stern warning for the things that I was accused of having said about him. I hadn't said anything about him except praising him for his pragmatic way of dealing with issues. About one week after the first warning, I was again summoned to his defunct office, this time, for a severe threat that he dubbed, the "last warning."

"Mr. Chitakure, I want to warn you about the things that you go around saying about me. Last week I told you not to talk about me. If you continue, I am going to kill you. I mean it. Yesterday, I could have shot you had it not been for your kids who came out to welcome you when you arrived at your house. I was hiding in the gum trees that are behind your house. You are playing with fire. Your gossiping should stop forthwith, or else, you will forever regret it." I knew that he wasn't joking.

"Brother, what did I say?" I earnestly inquired.

"You were celebrating my demotion," he answered.

"I celebrated your downfall? When?"

"Yesterday in the staffroom. You were singing, "*Ndiwe wakazvikanyira wega. Nyaya yako yekuzviidza gamba.*" (It *is* your own fault that you have been demoted. You thought that you were indomitable). "I want you to leave me alone. If you ever say anything about me, I will kill you." He hit the desk to emphasize his point.

"Brother, I never sang that song yesterday. I don't even know that you have been demoted. In fact, you are a good leader. I like you for many things. You don't procrastinate in your decision making. You don't vacillate like some leaders do. You stand by your promises. You instill discipline in the students. Whoever is feeding you these lies is looking for something. She is trying to create enmity between you and me."

"How do you know that it's a she? You should know that the walls have ears."

I knew who the malicious informer was. It was the Mathematics department head. She had been into the staffroom the previous day. Typically, she had her own staffroom, which was situated near the church. She had been angry with me because my friend with whom she was in love had ended the relationship. I also knew that her new boyfriend was the demoted deputy. Everyone at the college knew about their illicit affair. She is the one who had sung a Christian hymn in the staffroom on the day in question. Although I didn't know exactly why she would tell lies to Brother Charles, I reconstructed my own theory. Brother Charles was in love with three women at Kutama College, and it wasn't a secret. The Mathematics teacher knew that Brother Charles loved gossiping. So, whenever she needed him to come over to her house, she would promise him a juicy story, and if she didn't have one, she had to create one. By so doing, she would have a better share of the boyfriend than the other two women. That was my theory, and I shared it with Brother Charles, but he flatly denied it.

The accusation about me gossiping about him reminded me of the comments that Brother Charles had made about me at a ceremony that had been held at the college earlier that year. The former President of Zimbabwe, Mr. Robert G. Mugabe had donated two school buses to Kutama College. There was a handover ceremony at which all the teachers were presented to the former President. Since Bother Charles was the master of ceremonies, he had the privilege to say a few things about each teacher, as he/she came to the podium to greet the former President. When my turn came, he said, "This is Mr. John Chitakure, who teaches gossiping, I mean History." Later at the end of his long speech, the former President refuted Brother Charles. "Mr. Charles, as you listened to my life history, do you think it's gossiping? I say no—it's history. History is important." The President refuted him jokingly. So, the gossiping allegations had been gathering momentum for a while.

After my conversation with Brother Charles, I started thinking about the allegations seriously. Yes, he could have shot me. He had a gun. He was hiding in the gum trees behind my house. Yes, he was telling me the truth. He could still do it because his girlfriend would continue fabricating lies about me to attract his attention. Knowing the erratic and melodramatic behavior of this man, I decided to give his threat the benefit of the doubt. Suppose he was suffering from some mental health challenges, then I would die for nothing. My life was in danger. It was then when I decided to transfer from Kutama for my safety, and that of my family. Since changing schools wasn't as swift as I wanted, I had to go to Harare to solicit for protection from the brother's provincial leader. I was surprised that he wasn't shocked by the allegations that I presented. That awareness made me suspicious about him condoning the threats by his junior brother. Anyway, I was transferred to a high school that was about one mile from the College. The headmaster and the deputy head of this new school welcomed me warmly. That was Kutama Day High school, which was popularly known as Chimoto. I was asked to teach the English Language and History. Within a few weeks of being at Chimoto, I gained respect from both the students and teachers. I made new friends, some of whom have withstood the test of time. Sunny Seremani is one of them.

Kutama Day Secondary School

The working conditions at Chimoto were different from those at Kutama College. Some of the students were less talented yet were very eager to learn. I remained at Chimoto for a whole year. Soon, I discovered that some teachers at Chimoto weren't as committed to facilitating students' learning as most teachers at Kutama College. Some classes that were deemed incorrigible were neglected by the teachers. Some students were always tardy, and others would just abscond from school. I was different. I had brought the Kutama College work ethics and zeal to Chimoto, and some teachers reprimanded me.

"Chitakure, this isn't Kutama College. Why do you work so hard? How much do you earn for such hardworking? Or you want to be promoted to a higher post?" They teased me in their attempt to demoralize me, but I couldn't change my work ethic. I loved my job, and I respected students. The students liked my History classes. I later discovered that even the students who didn't belong to my Form Two History class would attend my classes without my knowledge since I didn't recognize every one of my students by face.

The Kutama Day High School was different in other ways. The teachers' house had two categories. There were the old houses, which only had electricity but lacked piped water and in-built bathrooms. Their occupants used Blair toilets or pit latrines. I got one of those houses. The senior teachers who had been teaching at Chimoto longer had modern brick-faced dwellings that had in-built bathrooms, electricity, and piped water. The school didn't provide additional incentives to the teachers apart from the salaries that they got from the government. But that was fine with me.

I was never lonely at Chimoto because my old friends from the college sometimes visited me to socialize at Chikambi Business Center. They also appraised me of the situation at the College. They told me that Brother Charles had finally left the office that he had refused to vacate when he was demoted. At that time, he was working at the hospital where he had already fallen out of favor of the patron of the hospital. At the end of 2005, he was forced to leave both the hospital and the college. I didn't sympathize with him for his misfortunes. As soon as I heard that he had left Kutama College, I wrote a letter to the head of Kutama College informing him of my intention to come back to the College. I did this for several reasons. First, to show my detractors at Kutama College, particularly the Mathematics teacher that the evil that people do come back to them. I also wanted Brother Charles' friends to know that I hadn't been expelled from Kutama, as the rumors had it, but that I had opted to leave for the sake of my safety.

Second, my sons were attending Kutama Day Primary School that was a stone's throw from the College. They would appreciate our going back to the college. They would as well reunite with their old friends at the school. At Chimoto, they never made any friends, since we traveled to and from Harare every weekend. Third, I always believed in the triumph of justice over injustice, oppression, and exploitation. I wanted it to be a lesson to other evil-minded people that you couldn't keep a good man down. The headmaster of Kutama College promptly responded to my letter and told me that I could come back to the college the following day. Yes, I went back to the Kutama College. I was so sad to leave my students and the new friends that I had made at Chimoto, but for the sake of my boys, I had to sacrifice them. I must say that my going back to the college affected my students to the extent that they resisted being taught by the new teacher that had been deployed to replace me.

So, I went back to Kutama College. Good had triumphed over evil, as had happened when the head of Magunje contemptuously refused to give me a teaching post at his school. There was another development that started when I was at Chimoto. I had been accepted by the Catholic Theological Union to study theology in Chicago, beginning in 2006. The application was finalized when I was back at Kutama College. So, in August of 2006, I resigned from the Ministry of Education, and I went to Chicago to begin my studies.

Summing Up

After all is said, you may want to know if I never talked about Brother Charles behind his back. I did, but not maliciously. He was our acting headmaster for about one year and acting deputy headmaster for over two years. He was a man in authority, and we couldn't avoid talking about him behind his back. Kutama College wasn't a concentration camp, so we were free to discuss issues and persons. For a person of Brother Charles' position, he would be naïve to imagine students and subordinates not talking about him behind his back. I spoke of him in his absence on numerous occasions. I openly told other teachers that he was a better leader than S. O. and that I preferred him than the incumbent headmaster.

Several traits made him admirable. First, he was pragmatic and frank. He was decisive and walked the talk most of the time. If a teacher asked him for permission to have an education or sporting trip with the students, Brother Charles would either allow the journey or deny the request, immediately. No dilly-dallying and shilly-shallying. S. O. was different. He would tell you to come back to his office at a later date, again and again, until you got tired of knocking on his door. He acted like he was doing the teacher and the students a great favor. With Brother Charles, there was no speculation about what you would have requested because he would tell you his decision there and then. For me, that was a great virtue because I am not good at persuading people to do the things that they should do, and are paid to do.

Second, Brother Charles was flexible in decision making. He listened to teachers and students' comments and promptly acted on them. On two occasions, he acted upon the advice that other teachers and I had given him. The first issue concerned the appointment of the senior master who was third in rank from the headmaster. A few of the teachers advised him to replace the one that held the position when we joined Kutama, with another one who was privy to the ethos of the Catholic traditions, and he made the change.

The second issue concerned the election of the school head boy. At most schools in Zimbabwe, the students and teachers choose a few student leaders, the most influential of whom are the head girl and head boy. Their primary task is to be intermediaries between the students and the staff. They have prefects working under them. In most schools, head boys and head girls are very powerful and influential in the administration of the school. They also have benefits that other students don't have. They eat better food and have better bedrooms. They are exempted from doing cleaning and other manual tasks. At Kutama, we only had the head boy because it was a "boys only" College. I always felt that the Kutama head boy had more authority than most ordinary teachers.

So, it happened that the students and the teachers elected a non-Catholic student as the head boy of Kutama, and some teachers and I felt that the position needed someone who knew the fundamental Catholic ethos since Kutama was a Catholic College. There was nothing segregative about the suggestions because that was the norm at all mission high schools, both Catholic and Protestant. Brother Charles refused to endorse the student in question, in favor of a Catholic candidate. The non-Catholic student became the deputy head boy, which wasn't a mean achievement, at Kutama College.

Third, Brother Charles was a Jack of all trades. He could drive a tractor, and the only means of student transport, which was a lorry called Bingo. When Kutama got its first two buses, Brother Charles became one of the designated drivers. He was generous too. Occasionally, he would throw a party for the teachers at which he entertained them with his killer dancing moves. He loved people and connected with them. I respected him for that.

Be that as it may, he had a dark side, just like all of us. He was a disciplinarian, who sometimes heavy-handedly meted out cruel punishments on misbehaving students. I witnessed him disciplining one of my senior students at the behest of his mother, and I couldn't hold back my tears. I had no authority to stop him because my responsibility as the student's class teacher was to merely witness him punishing the student. A couple of weeks after the incident, I tried to explain to him about how I felt about his treatment of the student, but he wouldn't listen. Despite his authoritarian way of disciplining students, most of them liked him.

Furthermore, most teachers found Brother Charles' moral disposition wanting in many respects, just like many of us. Most teachers felt that he was supposed to be different because he was a religious brother who had publicly professed vows of poverty, chastity, and celibacy. As I have already alluded to, Brother Charles was said to have three lovers at Kutama College. One of the women claimed to be married although I never met her husband. Two of them were teachers, and the third was one of the ancillary staff. Most residents and students knew about these illicit affairs because Brother Charles didn't try to hide them. Some non-Catholic staff members came to me complaining about Brother Charles' relations. Of the three women, two of them separately shared with me that they were in love with Brother Charles. One of them claimed that he was going to leave religious life, and marry her. I recall the nasty incident that one of the women alleged to have happened when Brother Charles, took the three women to a hotel.

However, I never gathered enough courage to verify the allegations with him until the last day he summoned me to his office. In fact, I told him about both sides of him, and he couldn't hide his astonishment about my positive comments. But he didn't refute the allegation about his public love affairs because they might have been accurate. These claims weren't news at Kutama because everyone knew about them. Even if I wanted to gossip about them, I wasn't going to find a willing listener because they weren't news at Kutama. I think that Brother Charles was conscious of the fact that everyone knew about his alleged affairs, but didn't bother.

I think that Brother Charles was frustrated to lose his position of power. I also felt sad for him because he was a good leader except for the few weaknesses that I outlined above, which had nothing to do with his dispensation of official duties. At the time of my interrogation, I wasn't aware that he had been demoted and that he was refusing to vacate the office. As a matter of fact, I learned about it from him when he accused me of spreading the rumors. It was after then when I shared the news with two friends who already knew about the demotion. Brother Charles had to find someone to vent his frustration on, and it happened to be a few of the teachers. Several of them were interrogated on the same day I was. What I don't understand was what Brother Charles intended to achieve by harassing teachers. His removal from office was irreversible. Since he wasn't officially employed by the government like all other teachers, he couldn't even appeal his dismissal. He was just wasting his time by refusing to retire.

On my last day at Kutama, we had a hearing at which Brother Charles denied that he ever threatened to kill me.

"Chitakure is a liar. I never threatened him. I never talked to him," Brother Charles contested fiercely. There were three of us—the headmaster, the new deputy head, and I.

I looked at him in the eyes and said, "Brother Charles, you have let me down. I always thought that you were invincible, and feared no man. I know you are a brave and honest man who speaks his mind. I feel let down because I was wrong about you. You are a liar. I never knew that you feared anyone." I paused.

"I thought that you would just say, "yes, I threatened to kill him. So what?" But you stand before the three of us, defending yourself by lying. I know that it's my word against yours, and considering the amount of influence you have, no one is bound to believe me. No one is going to believe that you told me that you were hiding in the gum trees near my house with your gun pointed at me. But I know that three persons know that I am speaking the truth—you, me, and God."

He stood up, paced the room, and angrily said, "I am going to do what I told you I would do." This was directed to the headmaster and his new deputy. The good headmaster jumped to his feet, and pleaded with him, "Please Brother, no. Please, no. Don't do it." I never got to know what he actually wanted to do. I guess one day I will be able to ask either the headmaster or his new deputy. When he calmed down, I bade them farewell and left for the Murombedzi District Education offices where I was assigned to Kutama Day Secondary School.

A Few Lessons

As I look back at this episode in my life, I derive some learning from it. It doesn't matter how well you speak of other people, they may still victimize you. Sometimes the people we accuse of gossiping are indeed innocent. We have to evaluate our sources, who may have hidden agendas for misleading us. People can use you to fight their own battles. I also learned that sometimes we make it too easy for abusers by opting to flee before we put up a fight. When I look back, I observe that I missed great opportunities in life because I didn't always choose to stand my ground, and force my opponent to earn their victory. I have more often found solace in quitting than fighting.

Again, like what I have already said above; this is my side of the story. Perhaps, Brother Charles has a different version of the same story. Unfortunately, until Brother Charles has an opportunity to present his side of the same story, the only version you have is mine. Until then, please, hold on to it.

CHAPTER 2

LET'S START FROM THE BEGINNING

Now, let's start from the beginning. I was born in 1973, perhaps five years after I was actually born. In fact, I really don't know when I was born. Please, don't think that I am foolish. I am not. My mother doesn't remember my birthday. She isn't stupid neither. I believe that there were worthier things to remember during my birth period than a child's birthday. This isn't a joke, just in case you think it is. However, I suspect that I was born in 1968, or thereabouts. Due to the War of Liberation of my country (Second Chimurenga), I began school late, and without a birth certificate. I wasn't the only student without a birth certificate at Chitakai Primary School. Most of my classmates had no birth certificates when we started school in 1980. Most of them eventually got birth certificates when we were in Grade Seven, in 1985. In that year, the school headmaster insisted that those who had no birth certificates wouldn't be allowed to write the Grade Seven examinations. In fact, he said that they wouldn't be allowed to "shade," which was a popular term in Zimbabwean primary schools during that time. The term "shading" came from the fact that all Grade Seven examinations had to be answered on a scantron form on which circles that corresponded to the most appropriate answers had to be shaded using an HB pencil only.

Yes, we were ready to "shade." We had waited for seven years for the opportunity to "shade," and no one was willing to let it slip through one's fingers because of having no birth certificate. The Grade Seven certificate was crucial because it would guarantee one's place in high school. For ethical reasons, my mother, probably in conspiracy with my class teacher and other parents, decided to subtract five years from my age. Do I have any evidence about that? The answer is "no." Although I have no evidence to support my guess, I have every reason to think that that might have been the case. It happened to most of my friends, and I don't see how I could have escaped it. In fact, some friends of mine, who had no birth certificates used their much younger brothers' birth certificates, and in the process, switched their names and ages. So, Walter became Farai. Jerius became Herbert.

A student's age was crucial because during Zimbabwe's colonial era (1890–1980) there was an age limit for the students who could be accepted into the few high schools that existed. Those students who didn't qualify to go to high school would be committed to the unskilled labor industries. The people didn't know that the new government of independent Zimbabwe would allow anybody who wanted education to be enrolled in high schools that the parents and the government would later build. The poorest of these high schools were known as "Upper Tops" for a reason I still don't know. Most of these schools were manned by unqualified teachers. Some of the few qualified teachers stationed at these schools were trained to teach at primary schools, not secondary schools. But due to the scarcity of teachers with relevant qualifications, teachers trained for primary education volunteered to assist at high schools. I have great respect for these teachers because they were well-meaning, diligent, industrious, and most of the time, intelligent.

During the war, most rural roads leading to towns were either destroyed or infested with mortar bombs, rendering them unusable. Parents couldn't travel to the nearest District offices (kwaMudzviti) to register their children's births or apply for birth certificates. When the war ended, people had ceased to care about birth certificates, and most never tried to obtain one until they were really needed. That's what the propaganda of a guerrilla warfare does. It makes you forget about the real future. It creates a utopian future in which happiness can be attained without sacrifices, hard work, and education.

Furthermore, most schools in Nyajena, except for one or two were closed or destroyed during the war. Consequently, the children who were supposed to start school during that period were delayed, some by more than five years. So, some students' ages were reduced when the parents finally had an opportunity or were compelled to officially certify the births of their children. But, this reduction was just a paper thing, because the actual ages remained the same. Consequently, most rural schools were full of young men and women, regarding birth records, who were trapped in older men and women's bodies. I shall return to this issue later.

The Sweetness of a New Name

I was born at Gaths Mine Hospital, in Mashaba, an asbestos mine near the then town of Fort Victoria, now Masvingo. That was at a time when Mashaba Mine was at its peak. I am not writing about the present day Mashaba, which has become like a ghost town, in which workers haven't received their wages for over a decade. I don't know the date of my birth, but my mother recalls that it was during the Easter Festival, and that earned me the name, Paschal. My mother, although literate, never cared to record the date of my birth, and I don't blame her for that. I don't know why, but I think that she lacked the wisdom that one day she would forget the date. That's what happens when one over-trusts her memory.

Paschal—a very nice and symbolic name, but fortunately or unfortunately, nobody ever called me by that name except my mother. My siblings knew it but never used it. All my friends weren't aware of it. Since we weren't Christians, I never thought that Paseka, as my mother pronounced it, was a unique and symbolic name. As I look at the appellation, Paseka, now, enlightened by all the theologies that I have studied throughout my academic life, I feel that although it sounds civilized, Christian, and uncommon, it's not a good name, symbolically, mainly when used in connection with the passion of Jesus Christ. Jesus' torture at the hands of his enemies was so devastating and disheartening that even those who had the foreknowledge about his future resurrection were traumatized by it. Although I have had enough share of challenges and blessings in this world, I wouldn't want to bear a name that reminds people of the heart-rending and nerve-racking trials and tribulations that Jesus experienced. I don't want to be the embodiment of that suffering. I shall return to this later.

Anyway, it's not helpful crying over a forgotten name that never was. As a matter of fact, people didn't run short of what to call me. My father called me Pagaravanhu. I don't know where he got that name from. It might have been my grandfather's name. Believe it or not, I never tried to trace its origin. Pagaravanhu—what a stupid and disastrous name! It is a compound name formed from two Shona words; *pagara* which comes from the verb *gara,* meaning, sit down, stay, live; and *vanhu*, which means, people. Hence, Pagaravanhu, or Pagaravantu, the variation that my father preferred, means where people stay.

My family and friends, except my grandmother who called me Pagara, shortened it to Paga. Although my grandmother and I weren't best friends, it seems that she felt drawn to me during the illness that led to her demise. "Pagara! Give me some water. Pagara wee! Go and fetch my medications." She would call out for me. I had become her caretaker and would go into the bushes to get the herbs that she instructed me to fetch for her. I still think that if she had been taken to the hospital, she might have survived the sickness. But, there were no hospitals because Muchibwa Hospital, the only one in Nyanjena, had been turned into an army barrack, by the Rhodesian soldiers. Mogenster Mission Hospital, which was run by the Dutch Reformed Church, and was about a hundred kilometers away from Machimbira's village, had become inaccessible because of the War. She died at home.

To many people, my name sounded like a nickname. That's why I never got a childhood nickname, for I already had one. Between my mother and father, I don't know who gave me that alienating name. I don't know why. I don't care about knowing because that name became a source of my childhood humiliation, embarrassment, and bullying. This was at a time when people could torment you because of your name. For many people, the name was strange. My friends laughed at me as if I had named myself. I come between a brother and sister, and they both have better names. My brother's name is Emmanuel. It's a good Christian name, although he has never attempted to become one. My sister's name is Emilia— another beautiful name of Latin origin. I don't understand why my parents decided to insert the name Pagaravanhu between Emmanuel and Emilia. The name could have come from a song that my family and I listened to as I was growing up. Its title was "Pagala bantu." It could be that the song was bought in honor of my name. Wherever the name came from, I didn't like it.

Then one day I got so tired of shame, and I changed my name. That's one of the many advantages of not having a birth certificate. I named myself, John. It was a better name. It was a civilized name. It was English too. Also, it was a Christian name, as I came to learn later. I loved it. My teachers and friends loved it as well. Do you want to know how it happened? One day, as my First-Grade teacher was about to call the class attendance register, I walked to where he was and told him that I wanted to change my name to John Tsaurai. Tsaurai was my uncle's first name, which his children and I used as our last name when we were in primary school. Changing my name was a heroic act. Indeed, it was a revolution. I had spent one week gathering enough energy to do that. I was prepared for whatever the teacher would say. He agreed. No question was asked. As the names were being called out on that Monday morning, for the first time, I answered to a new name. It felt terrific. I had removed the burden of shame that I had carried since birth. My friends looked at me in puzzlement, but they were happy too. From that day on, I became John. That marked the end of the shame, pain, and the persecution that my original name had caused me.

You may wonder why I changed my name at that point in my life. The bullying had become unbearable because so many students at Chitakai Primary School were hearing it for the first time. Before I started school in 1980, my friends had become accustomed to my name, and they rarely laughed at me. It was different when I started Grade One. Every time I introduced myself to a teacher or a classmate, those around would burst into laughter. "What sort of a name is that? Is it a nickname?" They would ask. "What does it mean?" They would torment me. You may imagine how it felt to try to convince the whole school that Pagaravanhu was my real name, not my nickname. It feels better to be ridiculed for a mistake that you have committed rather than a name, which your parents gave you.

If your country has never been colonized by anyone, you may not understand why a name may cause a lot of embarrassment to its bearer. The most damaging and enduring aspect of colonization is psychological. Psychological domination compels the vanquished to undermine their own values, religious traditions, and thought patterns. In other words, the culture of the dominated people is demonized, again and again, until it looks evil. For the colonized people to feel more acceptable to their colonizers, they may try to assimilate the new way of life. Some run away from their food, hair texture, clothes, songs, rituals, medicines, and names, in order to feel civilized, and more acceptable to their rulers. Those who assimilate to the new culture may begin to belittle those who continue to follow the indigenous culture. They perceive them as old-fashioned and too traditional. They are the SRBs people (Strong rural background people).

In Zimbabwe, the acquisition of that so-called civilization was reflected in many spheres of life, including the names the parents gave to their children. Civilized parents would give their children European names. So, to many other people and me, the name John, was more refined and acceptable than Pagaravanhu. Yes, people may revolt against geographic and economic colonization but may remain captives of the psychological effects of that domination for many years. Only sacrifices and the cultivation of self-esteem may liberate one from the mental colonization.

My mother never denied me the sweetness of naming myself. I guess, she knew that Pagaravanhu wasn't a lovely name. Yes, she called me Paseka, but she never insisted that everyone called me by that name. As it happened, only one person regretted my name change. It was my uncle, Tsaurai, whose nickname, Chovurombo, had become like his first name. At that time, he was my guardian. One weekend, he came back from Triangle, where he was working to find out that I had changed my name. He said, "Nephew, why did you change your name? Your name, Pagaravanhu, is unique. Certainly, it's a special name. John isn't a good name because too many people have it. Some of them are thieves and failures in life." He was right because I knew about ten people who were named John. Some of them were very successful, but others, not so glorious. My uncle was the first person ever to tell me that Pagaravanhu was indeed a good name. Nobody else had ever said that to me. In any case, it was too late and painful to go back to Pagaravanhu. That name had been a source of my ridicule throughout my childhood. I had managed to kill it. I had buried it. It was an achievement. And it gave me much relief.

As I reflect on that name now, I feel that my uncle was right. Pagaravanhu is a unique and significant name. This feeling might be a result of the onset of old age. When people become older, they tend to embrace the reality that they would have spent the better part of their lives trying to evade. Most people begin to cherish the family traditions that they used to condemn. They become humble enough to allow the wisdom of the elders to hold them by the hand and lead them wherever it deems suitable. They begin to perceive certain things differently from the way they used to view them when they were younger. Most start to realize that at times you conquer the world by being patient and forgiving, not by impatience and war. They stop being irritated by the things that used to drive them mad when they were younger. Most begin to see the value of their culture and start to regret the time they would have wasted pursuing the lifestyles of others. They begin to understand and appreciate the importance of the ancestral wisdom and curse themselves for not having amassed as much of it as was available. They start to taste the sweetness of the water from their own wells, rather than wasting time chasing after the forbidden waters from other people's springs. They begin to realize the health benefits of eating their own indigenous foods, instead of pursuing refined foods from different cultures. It has dawned on me that there was nothing wrong with the name, but something was wrong with those people who ridiculed and bullied me because of it. I regret the sleepless nights that I spent worrying about the appellation instead of studying.

With hindsight, if I had been asked to choose between the names, John and Paschal, I would have preferred John. Although the word paschal has more to do with Easter than Good Friday, there is no Easter without Good Friday. If I decide to embrace Easter, I can't avoid embracing Good Friday, as well. But, I don't want Good Friday. I don't want to suffer. I wish my whole life were Easter Sunday, full of celebration and victory over all evil machinations. I want to be happy. I want to attain prosperity. I want to have good health. And I want a long life. The name Paschal would have been a constant reminder that suffering is an inescapable part of life. We all know that, and we don't want to be reminded of it. So, I am happy that I went for the name John, instead of Paschal.

Of course, if I had been given another opportunity to choose between the names Paschal and Pagaravanhu, I would have gone for Paschal. Although the name Paschal is related to the passion and resurrection of our Lord Jesus Christ, for me, Pagaravanhu was the passion itself. You can imagine what people would be calling me now, with the controversial South African dancer, Zodwa wabantu. I think that some of my friends were going to taunt me by calling me, Paga wabantu. I can imagine, some people asking me if I were related to her, or if I also walked around without underwear. For those who have never heard of Zodwa—she is a South African celebrity, who means no harm to anyone, but claims to walk around without underwear. I think that there is nothing unique about not wearing underwear except that Zodwa tells people about it. I guess that many other people do the same, either by choice or poverty, but they don't preach about it.

My Runaway Father

My father's name was David Masika. You can see for yourself the hypocrisy of some parents. His parents had named him David; a very biblical and beautiful name, yet he thought of no other fitting name for me except Pagaravanhu. I am not sure if he was born in Zimbabwe or Mozambique, but that doesn't matter. I want to believe that he was born in Zimbabwe, in Chimanimani, in chief Mutambara's area, and then migrated to Mozambique. As a matter of fact, I don't know much about him or his family because we never visited them. His totem is Shumba of the sub-totem Sigauke. I don't know where he met my mother, and I don't want to know. Those are some of the things Shona children never ask from their parents. Perhaps they met at Mashaba Mine where my father was working. My mother had had a divorce from another man, with whom she had mothered three children—two boys and one girl. I think she deemed herself lucky to find a young man who was willing to marry a divorcee. The Shona people discourage single men from marrying single mothers although there are no hard and fast rules about that. Many young men have always ignored that tradition.

I don't recall what my father looked like. There are no pictures of him although I remember photos of all of us being taken when I was a kid. It could be that he took all the pictures with him when he left. However, I have a few sweet memories of my father. My brother, Emmanuel and I used to wait for him on his way back from work. He was a miner. Usually, he brought us some cold tea and hard bread, which we called, *chitumbuwa*. The bread was intended to be a lifeline to the miners if, because of one reason or another, they were trapped underground. My father neither drank his tea nor ate his bread. He would bring them home after every work shift. I don't know why he neither consumed his bread nor drank his tea. It could have been that he felt that we appreciated the hard bread and tea more than he did, or that he was never hungry because he never got trapped underground.

I also remember the times when my father would cut my hair at the water tank near our house. By the end of every hair-cutting episode, he would be so irritated because of my never-ending fidgeting. Although I can't remember it, I might have received a few slaps for that. In any event, we were great friends. When my father got injured in the mine, I remember spending a night or two with him at the mine hospital, which I thought was so cool. Even when I later returned home, leaving him in the hospital, my brother and I still visited him every morning to see him, and also to drink free fresh milk, which the mine provided for all patients. Of course, we would take some back home to our mother who would be eagerly waiting for it.
I also recall my father buying us some spectacular belts. They were magnificent because their buckles changed color when tilted. Those straps were no mean feat at a time when most children of my age walked around in tattered clothes that showed their bare bottoms. At that time, buying straps for children was considered a sheer waste of money. I will never forget those straps because they made us famous, for every kid wanted to hold the mesmerizing buckles.

Then my father vanished. Of course, his disappearance wasn't political because political disappearances weren't yet known. His was a disappearance that was driven by his irresponsible attitude. The best word to describe his action would be "abandonment." He abandoned us. The four of us. Just like that. I don't understand what goes on in the mind of a man, who fathers four children, loves them, and then vanishes.

He had a dark side too. "My father was a heavyweight boxing champion. He had an insatiable passion for the game. Already within the first round of the fight, he would make sure that his opponent was knocked down two or three times in a row. Unlike professional boxers, my father had no rules governing him; he had no referee, and consequently, he would not stop boxing his opponent, despite the pleas and cries for mercy from the opponent. He kicked, shoved, slapped, punched, arm-twisted, thrashed, and cursed the half-dead opponent. The "great" fighter in him would not stop until the opponent fainted, or pretended to do so. He could have become the world heavyweight boxing champion, but unfortunately or fortunately, he never challenged and never had any other opponents but one; because he knew that he would never lose the fight since the adversary never fought back and that opponent was none other than my poor mother!

My brother and I would stand there crying helplessly, witnessing the brutality in its totality. I was about four years old, but my mother's cries still remain vivid and fresh in my mind. I always remember how my mother, my bother, and I would then go to a particular church, or whatever it was, in the middle of the night and would sleep there on the veranda. Sometimes my mother would knock on the church door, even though she knew that the door was locked and that there was no one living there. Perhaps she thought that God would open the door for us, or maybe it was merely the confused action of a battered, dehumanized, and humiliated woman.

That was around the year 1977 in a small mining compound of Mashava, in Zimbabwe. My mother is lucky to be a survivor of domestic violence because God intervened. My father just disappeared around 1977, never to be seen again. My mother is still alive, but she still bears the marks of the brutal attacks she endured stoically. We never mention my father when we gather as a family, and whenever his name is mentioned accidentally, a current of pain passes between my mother and those of us who witnessed the atrocities of a heavyweight boxing champion who never was."[1]

I don't know how my mother found out that he had gone. What I remember is that we had gone to our mother's rural home, as we always did, and he was gone. I don't think he ever said goodbye to anyone. I don't know what happened to the household property that was in our Gaths Mine house. In fact, it was just a room; not a house. The room was only big enough for a bed, wardrobe, and a paraffin stove. All that we came to know was that he ran away with another woman, who was at that

---

[1] John Chitakure. *Shona Women in Zimbabwe—A Purchased People.* Eugene, Oregon: Wipf and Stock, 2016, 1–2.

time pregnant with his child. I recall that woman living with us in that small room. She was a very dark-skinned woman, but beautiful in her own way. Rumors have it that they resettled in Mozambique where they had another child, this time, a girl. I met that girl once when she came visiting my mother in the late 90s. She passed away in 2013. I never met my step-brother, who I think is still alive, living somewhere in Zimbabwe.

Before he went away, our standard of life was high. We lived in a mining compound where we had tap water. We had a radio. The mine screened free movies for the miners and their families every Saturday night. Our hero was Jack. We had good food and beautiful clothes. Then all that was gone. We all suffered because of my father's departure. We also didn't know what had happened to him. Was he dead or alive? As time went on, and there was no word about him, we ceased to care. We knew that he had gone for good. I was devastated. When you are a kid, it feels good to have a father even if he is a fool or bully.

Although I have some fond memories of him, most of them have been overshadowed by his final act of cowardice—abandoning us. Have I forgiven him? Yes, a thousand times. Does forgiveness mean that I should now go looking for him like Uncle Chovurombo did? Never. Does it mean that I should forget his final act to us? No. For me, forgiveness means that I remember all the pain that he caused us. I sustain the wounds his irresponsible behavior inflicted on us. I don't wish to forget that. It's part of my identity. But, I don't want any harm to happen to him because of what he did to us. But I will never go looking for him. I am not the type of a person who goes around begging some irresponsible man to become my father. Even if I were to find him now, there is nothing he can possibly do for me that other people haven't done for me in his absence.

Perhaps, the way I narrated my mother's ordeal, and how she stoically endured the battering from my father presents my mother as a hero, but most women, who lived during that era know that wife battering wasn't one woman's ordeal. Many women were and are still victims and survivors of domestic violence. Domestic violence is a universal social cancer that doesn't discriminate people because of race, nationality, color, social class, and so on. I think that the knowledge of not being alone makes every victim of domestic abuse braver. For many people, it feels better to know that you are not alone in your suffering. My mother wasn't alone. My mother is luckier because she survived, and I can narrate her story. There are myriads of women who have been subjected to more abuse than my mother but have no one to tell their stories. Some have died from that violence, and others continue to suffer in silence.

When we were kids, we shuttled between Mashaba Mine and Nyajena, where our mother's relatives lived. We never came to know any of my father's family. Of course, he had friends and distant relatives who also worked at Mashaba, but they weren't his close relatives. I knew Uncle VaKugurira, who lived at Temeria and ended up in Zvishavane where he later died. My brother, Emmanuel spent some time with him in Zvishavane in the late 70s. I knew uncle Basopo, who also lived in Gaths Mine, kuChikomburasi. I visited him in the early 90s at Mashaba and felt that he was cold and distant. There was my father's nephew, who ran a barber shop at Temeria. But, these were more of my father's friends than relatives. Our relationship with them ended when my father left. We were lonely.

In the Shona culture, it's sad not to know one's relatives, especially from the father's side. It was another cause of our ridicule as we grew up in my mother's home village. We were referred to as the "fatherless children." Some people would call us, "Manyasarandi," which was a derogatory term used for people who had migrated to Zimbabwe from Nyasaland (Malawi). The worst name was *makora* (wild cats). A feral cat is known for its nefarious activities. It steals chickens from people's homes. It comes at night and impregnates the domestic cat. No one gets to see or know it. The kittens may vaguely know their iniquitous father when he pays their mother some nocturnal visits, but they never experience his fatherly care. The Shona found the term *makora* appropriate for children whose father isn't legally recognized.

Uncle Savious and the Winds of Destruction

After my father went away, we went to live with my mother's family in Nyajena. There was nothing unusual about it because we had always gone there to visit, sometimes for extended periods. However, this time it was different because our stay would be permanent. Initially, we lived in my grandmother's large round hut, which was used as a kitchen, sitting, and dining room. Later, my grandmother felt that we needed to build our own house, in her backyard. Or it could be that my mother, just wanting a bit of freedom, and sought permission to construct her own hut. Mother wasn't asking for an impossible favor because the land was available. Grandmother had a large piece of land, which she used for farming. My mother's sister, Maiguru Mai Fungi, already had a home in the same backyard.

When the permission was granted as was expected, my mother hired Uncle Absalom Mutinha to construct a round hut for us. Uncle Absalom is one of the several young men from Machimbira's village who joined the War of Liberation in the early 70s and never came back home at independence. No one in their families knows what happened to them. For many years, their parents and siblings expected to see them alive, knocking on the door, one of the days. They never did. Up to date, there hasn't been any closure for their families. The only logical conclusion that their relatives drew was that they might have perished during the War. Many people did.

Mother's hut was never finished, not because Uncle Absalom went to War before he completed the job, but because the winds of destruction arose, as they sometimes did during those years. The hostile winds had found a natural and willing host in Uncle Savious, my mother's brother, or stepbrother, or whatever she called him. I am not sure of his age at that time; maybe he was in his early twenties. He was the last born in my mother's family and was still living with my grandmother. At that time, he was not married. As a matter of fact, he never did.

Uncle Savious had two diametrically opposed personalities. On the one hand, he could be an adorable man if he chose to. It's only that most of the time he opted to appease his vicious demons. He was an accomplished hunter and fisherman. Occasionally, he brought home lots of fish and game meat. We loved him for that. He was also an accomplished dancer. We liked his dancing moves and imitated him when we were playing with other kids. Furthermore, he was a hard worker, whenever he chose to work in grandmother's field. There was always enough food for the family. On top of that, he was an accomplished singer, who never composed new songs, but just remixed old ones. He gave the old popular songs a personal touch that completely transformed them, and never failed to inspire his audience. As if those were not enough talents, Uncle Savious was a passionate story-teller, who spiced his stories with songs and dances. I am referring to a period when there were no radios and television sets that could be used for entertainment. The few novels that were on the market were exorbitant and beyond ordinary people's pockets. So, Uncle Savious became the family's source of entertainment.

On the other hand, Uncle Savious could opt to be egregious from time to time. In actuality, in those times, he was like the quintessence of the devil. He was a bully who could just punish you for no apparent reason. He had unchecked power, which he abused whenever he decided to. Most of the time, he would come back home from drinking sprees at night. We always knew when he was about to arrive home—he sang. My grandmother would instruct us to pretend to be sleeping, just before he entered the house. Of course, pretending to sleep never appeased his abusive demons. He would wake us up, at times, with a whip, to the chagrin of Grandmother, who had no power to restrain him. We would wake up and clap hands for him while he sang and danced until he got tired. It's not that we didn't enjoy his feats of entertainment; we did. What we detested was the manner in which it was done, and the punishment that was meted out to those who didn't pretend to enjoy it the way he expected.

Even my grandmother was afraid of him. He is the guy who would go beer drinking for a week or two without coming back home. When he finally did return home, he would demand all the food that he could have consumed if he were at home. When my grandmother failed to meet his unrealistic demands, he would threaten to burn all of us in the hut. Thank God, he never did. I think that at some point, he tried but was not successful. His failure to set the hut on fire could have been a result of him not wanting to do it, or being too drunk to ignite the fire. In times like that, grandmother would call for help at the top of her voice. Her other son, Uncle Chovurombo would come to our rescue, but not without engaging in a small fracas with Uncle Savious. Surprisingly, when grandmother noticed that Uncle Savious was in trouble, she would intervene in support of her last born. That timely intervention by Uncle Chovurombo was good enough to temporarily exorcize Uncle Savious' demons. For a week or so, he would be his very best self. That was Uncle Savious.

Let me go back to my mother's hut. One evening, Uncle Savious came back home from one of his never-ending beer drinking sprees and destroyed my mother's almost finished shelter with his ax. Single-handedly, he razed it to the ground. It was like the Zimbabwean Operation *Murambatsvina*. For those who may not have heard about Operation *Murambasvina* (clear the filth); it was launched by the government of Zimbabwe in May 2005, with the intention of destroying all illegal structures in the capital city, Harare. By the time it was stopped, many people had become homeless. Uncle Savious' operation was a one-man *Murambasvina*. He was unstoppable. He demolished the round hut to the ground, pole by pole. *Sekuru* (Uncle) Absalom tried to talk him out of it, but *Sekuru* Savious was beyond any logic. He contemptuously refused to be drawn into a dialogue. He was also above the law. Indeed, he was the law itself.

As he dismantled the hut on that fateful day, he was cursing. He said that he was tearing down the shelter because he didn't want *makora* (feral cats) in his mother's premises. *Makora* refers to children who are born without the proper marriage processes between their father and mother being followed. Usually, the derogatory term is used by a mother's relatives about the children that she brings with her after divorce. In this instance, *makora* referred to my siblings and I. If you have never been called *gora* (singular form of *makora*) in your life, you may not have the idea of how it feels to be named one. It's utterly demeaning and dehumanizing. It hurts, not only for one day but for a very long time. It saps all your self-esteem from you. It reminds you of how worthless you are. It makes you feel like you are just an animal, not a good one, but a thieving and fornicating one. It reminds you that you don't belong, and you are not welcome. Being called a *gora* is not one of the insults you are likely to forget as long as you live. That's what Uncle Savious called us, not once, but on countless occasions.

I don't know how mother felt about the demolition of her hut, but I think she was devastated. I don't want to ask her about it because this issue is one of the many tribulations that we never discuss without provoking some hidden grief. But, Uncle

Savious being her brother, she might have expected it. I also think that she found it easier to forgive him.

As I look at it now, I feel that Uncle Savious was the real *gora*, not us. He was a dubious character, alcoholic, bully, and conman. He never got married. He never fathered a kid. Of course, not one that we know of. He once told me that his primary concern was about finding money to buy beer, not to raise a family. He didn't want to have any responsibility in life. He never built a home. He never owned even a chicken. At some point, he claimed to have fathered a kid, whose name he claimed to be "Thanks." Initially, we believed it, but it turned out that Thanks only existed in his imagination. As might be expected, he gained something from that sterile imagination—people started calling him *baba* Thanks (father of Thanks). Everyone knew that Thanks never was, but the name sounded funny. It became one of his many nicknames, which included VaBee, VaKusadha, VaNduna, and others that depicted his inflated ego.

Despite all his shortcomings, we always loved him. There was something about him that made him enchanting. The same may be correct about the relationship between many abusers and their victims. Instead of resenting the abusers, some of their victims adore them. We also learned a few lessons from *Sekuru* Savious. Anybody who lived with him had to learn the art of forgiveness because Uncle Savious always needed an abundance of it. The relatives that he conned of their valuables still gave him another chance. At some point, he conned Uncle Chovurombo of his hard-earned cash and ran away. He came back a couple of years later, and Uncle Chovurombo never hesitated to reconcile with him. At another point, he came to live with us in our own home, and nobody reminded him of his past actions.

He then disappeared for a very long time. The last time I saw him was in 1988, or thereabouts, before he went away, only to come back in 2004. When he returned from wherever he had been, he was sick and dying. I went home to see him and found him already dead and buried. My mother told me that when he came back home, he was a changed man. Life had humbled him. Yes, it does. He had become a shadow of himself. Mother recalls when Uncle Savious asked her to purchase a knife for him. She did. Yes, she bought a knife for a dying man. I still wonder why a man on a deathbed would need a knife. When my mother asked him why he needed a knife, he is said to have responded. "*Vatete, hazvina kunaka kuti munhu wemurume agare asina banga. Ko kana matsotsi akauya ndinomagwisa neyi?*" (My sister, a man, should have a weapon (knife) with which to fight robbers if they come). It's incredible that his deathbed had taught him to be responsible to the extent of wanting to protect his sister from robbers; the same sister, my uncle made vulnerable by razing her only hut to the ground. Yes, he needed a knife. As an avid hunter, he might have been thinking of plying his trade in the ancestral world.

Ironically, he died in my mother's arms. That's what *karma* does. In your weaker moments, it brings you into contact with people you used to despise, for you to taste how it feels to have no power. We miss Uncle Savious. Whenever all my family members who knew him gather, we talk and laugh about him. Ironically, we all love and miss him.

Childhood Friends

I had many childhood friends some of whom I don't recall by names. I will mention a few of them here. Jephias Mutinha and his brother, Hosea, were the closest of all my friends. We went to school and church together. We played soccer together. We talked, laughed, and at times, cried together. They were like brothers to me. It's sad that both died in circumstances that were very sad. Both probably got the pauper's burials in Harare. It was so sad, indeed. We belonged to very low-income families. We were distant relatives. Their father was my mother's uncle and had been a migrant worker in South Africa. He got married in South Africa and raised his children there. Then, one year, he brought his family back to Zimbabwe. His wife was South African. They had seven children in South Africa, and three more in Zimbabwe. Both Jephias and Hosea were hard workers in school, but their toils were never rewarded. Both had big dreams that they never realized.

I had other friends, as well, and I am not at liberty to mention them by names. One of them got entangled with a senior woman, who was older than his own mother. He was madly in love with her that no advice could persuade him to leave her. At some point, he is said to have squandered his school fees and ran away from school. He started drinking. He stopped going to church. Then tragedy befell him. He died an unfortunate death. He got involved in a fistfight at a beer party, and his adversary stabbed him with a knife. He died young. His mother was devastated. We were pained, and we learned a few lessons from his premature demise.

There was also another friend of mine who became involved in adult things before some of us did. He started drinking alcoholic beverages, smoking cigarettes, and indulging in sex at a tender age. Whenever we were walking to school, he would narrate to us the sacred paths he had walked and the forbidden springs from which he had drunk. Listening to his adventures was like watching a pornographic movie. He was very athletic and handsome, and girls loved him. After completing Ordinary Level at Mudarikwa High School, he went to Harare, got married, only to come back in a coffin a few years later.

Another friend of mine changed names when we were seniors in high school. He was a tall and skinny boy. He was much disciplined than most of us, and never got involved in any unapproved activities. He was a friend one could trust. He was very loyal. He wasn't involved in any extracurricular activities at school. He was hardworking in his studies, though less talented academically. He didn't have a girlfriend in high school and never looked for one. He loved his church and God. After high school, he went to town. Later, he came back and got married. He had two children when his wife died. He remarried and is now working in one of the small towns in Zimbabwe.

The Magnanimous Uncle Chovurombo

There were many heroes in my life, but at this juncture, I shall tell you about only one of them, Uncle Tsaurai, whose nickname was Chovurombo. *Chovurombo* is a Shona noun, which comes from the verb, *vurombo,* meaning poverty, and the prefix *che*, which designates ownership. Hence, *chovurombo* means the owner of poverty or the impoverished one. He earned this nickname from the utter poverty in which he grew up. I have every reason to think that he led a miserable life as a kid, perhaps just like most kids of his generation. My grandmother was a widow, and that might have compounded my uncle's tribulations.

To worsen the matter, Uncle Chovurombo was not my grandfather's son. He was a *"gora"* like me. When my grandfather died, my grandmother had an affair with another man—a stranger, and the result of that relationship was Uncle Chovurombo. So, he grew up in the Chitakure family as an illegal child since his father hadn't paid bridewealth for my grandmother. I guess Uncle Chovurombo's childhood wasn't comfortable. After him, my grandmother had her last born, *Sekuru* Savious. Savious' father was my late grandfather's younger brother, who was authorized to inherit my grandmother if he wanted to. Uncle Chovurombo was the only odd one in a family of six. I think that his half-brothers and sisters loved him and treated him well, although that couldn't take away the stigma of being an illegitimate child. I can imagine the shame and embarrassment that he might have experienced in his childhood and early adulthood.

I do understand why one morning, in the early 80s, we woke up to the joyful gathering, which was a family party to welcome his biological father. Uncle Chovurombo had hunted down his father and found him at some place near Renco Mine. He brought him home amid graceful jubilation and smiles. Although his father was happy to see his son finally, Uncle Chovurombo was much happier to find someone to call father, at long last. For him, his wife, and six or seven children, it was a tremendous victory, which was as therapeutic as buying underwear. His father's arrival was like a cleansing ritual. At last, my uncle had managed to remove the stigma of being a fatherless child or parent. His children, at long last, had a grandfather. His wife now had a father-in-law. I was a little jealous because I became the only one in that gathering who didn't have a father. Before the arrival of Uncle Chovurombo's father (VaChidharabhoyi), my uncle and I had implicitly shared the shame of being *makora* in the family. His children were not *makora* because they had a legally recognized father. His wife was not a *gora* because she had a father. Only the two of us were. I am not surprised that he never called me a *gora*. Yes, he wouldn't do that without him experiencing the same pain that I would feel whenever someone called me a *gora*.

The arrival of VaChidharabhoyi changed everything. My uncle and his children didn't waste time. They quickly changed their last name from Tsaurai to VaChidharabhoyi's official name. I was the only one who got stuck with Tsaurai as my last name because I couldn't change it to my uncle's new last name. I switched my last name to Chitakure when I was in Grade Four or Six. At primary school, I benefitted from using Tsaurai as my last name because my uncle always paid building fund on time. My mother paid it very late if she ever paid it at all. So, when kids whose parents hadn't yet paid building fund were being sent away from school, I was spared because I was a Tsaurai.

My uncle's father, who we had nicknamed, VaChidharabhoyi, because of his penchant for short trousers enjoyed his new home and worked hard in the fields. At that time, he was in his late 70s or early 80s and seemed to have become a shadow of himself. His strength was slipping away because of old age. He was serendipitous to have found someone to take care of him in his old age. He was a little jealous of his newly discovered son too. He sometimes reminded me that I had no right to receive gifts from his son, meaning my very Uncle Chovurombo, because I wasn't his child. He talked like he had contributed something to what his son had become. I just shrugged off his comments because I knew that he too had no right to receive gifts from a son he had never cared for. I am not sure if he had met my uncle before coming to live with him.

However, VaChidharabhoyi's honeymoon was short-lived because one evening, at least two years after his arrival, he was kicked out. I don't know the crimes that he had committed that warranted his expulsion from his new home, but they must have been unforgivable. He shamefully and unceremoniously walked away, carrying the same bag that he had brought when he first arrived. The bag was full of his *mvuto* (a fan made of baboon skin that is used to supply oxygen to the fire when heating metals to produce tools). I can't imagine how he felt, to be banished by the son who had searched for him all his life. To him, it might have felt like a betrayal of the highest level, but for my uncle's family, his dismissal might have tasted like sweet revenge. He got a taste of his own medicine. He had lived an irresponsible life, and nobody was going to be accountable for his. He retraced his footsteps back to the place where he had come from. Yes, he left, and no one missed him. Maybe my uncle did, but he never shared that with anyone. VaChidharabhoyi later died, and I don't know where and how. He had contributed nothing to my uncle's well-being and left him nothing when he was ostracized. The only indelible traces of his identity that he left were his name and totem. I wish his soul a peaceful rest.

As I continue to reflect on Uncle Chovurombo's father's coming to live with my uncle and his subsequent dismissal, I learn a few things. First, there is nothing that a biological father, who comes into your life when you are already an adult, can do to improve your life. In fact, he may worsen it because he too needs to be cared for. My uncle was happy to find his father, prove that he wasn't fatherless, and get a legal last name, but he discovered that there was nothing more to that. Second, a father who doesn't take care of his child is as bad as having no father at all. There is nothing he can do to help an adult son, which his guardians wouldn't have done for him. Third, it's tough to get to know and be connected to a Johnny-come-lately dad. Finally, if he isn't Bill Gates or Strive Masiiwa, he becomes an unnecessary financial burden to carry. Uncle Chovurombo's father left, and life continued as before. My advice to reckless or divorced parents is that, please, take care of your children if you want them to do the same to you in time of your need. Don't just appear later in their lives and expect to enjoy the emotional connection that is supposed to be shared between caring parents and their children.

Anyway, let me go back to my good Uncle Chovurombo. He grew up to be very wise. I admire him for having overcome all the poverty of his childhood to become the man he is now. He got married when he was about 20 years old. He was lucky because he married a hardworking, kind-hearted, and generous woman. Although he talks about his childhood poverty, when I was growing up, he was no longer poor. The only remnant of his childhood poverty is his nickname, Chovurombo. I only know him as one of the wealthiest persons in Machimbira's village. One day I asked him, "*Sekuru*, why did they give you the nickname, Chevurombo?"

He replied, "*Muzukuru*, I was one of the poorest children at Chitakai Primary School when I was growing up. I didn't have appropriate clothes to wear to school. Of course, most students had the same challenge, but mine was worse. The only decent clothing I could wear to school was my mother's woolen jersey. It was red. My mother and I shared it. Whoever got it first, was its owner on that particular day. Your grandmother, like other women of her age, had taken to the habit of beer drinking, and that brought a big conflict of interest to our jersey sharing arrangement. She had to wait for me to come back from school so that she would take over her jersey and wear it to beer parties. There were days when she wouldn't come back home from beer parties, and I had to miss school because I had no other shirt to wear to school. We waited for each other. She waited for me to come back from school, and I waited for her to come back from the beer party. At school, I played soccer, and my teammates and other students nicknamed me, Chevurombo."

I think that Uncle Chovurombo's childhood poverty gave him the discipline and wisdom that molded the person he became. Of course, I am not taking anything away from the training his half-brothers (Kallepa and Kallipos) might have instilled in him. I am also not taking anything away from the wisdom that might have come from his wife. Uncle Chovurombo is the one who came to our rescue when Uncle Savious demolished my mother's hut when it was still under construction. He offered us a place to build our shelter in his own premises. I don't think he did that because of the love he had for his sister—my mother, but because of his empathy for us, the kids. He knew the insecurities and vulnerabilities of having no father and that of being called a wildcat.

Uncle Chovurombo also had a good heart. After the demise of my mother's two brothers, Kallepa and Kallipos, he assumed the position of the family peacemaker. He is the person who occasionally rescued all of us, including my grandmother, whenever Uncle Savious went berserk. Uncle Savious could run amok at any time that he chose, but knowing that Uncle Chovurombo would come to our aid, gave us great relief. It also gave us the courage to grin and bear the cruelty of a reckless bully stoically. I have mentioned Uncle Savious trying to burn all of us in my grandmother's house, at some point. In situations like that Uncle Chovurombo would intervene, at times, heavy-handedly, to the displeasure of my grandmother.

Uncle Chevurombo, though barely literate, was full of wisdom as I have already mentioned. Why do I think so? He did the right things at the right time. He married a very energetic, big-hearted, and kind woman. She bore him many children, adorable and God-fearing people. His wife toiled in the fields to produce food for the family. Although Uncle Chevurombo was working in Triangle where he got a meager salary, there was always enough food for the family. In his teen years, he had trained to be a tailor. He bought an expensive sewing machine which he used to sew his children's clothes. He purchased a wheelbarrow, which wasn't a mean achievement during that time. He had other household tools, such as shovels, picks, pincers, and many others that distinguished him from mere mortals. He bought cattle that gave his family milk, manure, and plowing power. He had a bicycle, which at that time, was an essential and valuable mode of transport. He was what every decent man would dream of becoming.

He was one of the few villagers in Machimbira's village who owned a radio. Every evening, we would gather at his place, listening to radio programs. Local dramas, musical programs such as *Makwikwi emagitare*, and the reading of novels were popular radio programs during that time. He owned a Scotch cart, which was a necessity for carrying agricultural produce from the fields. He had goats and donkeys. My uncle was the first person in the village to buy a television set. Once per week, we would gather at his home to watch wrestling and the most households' favorite musical TV show called *Ezomgido*.

Whenever I think of him, the first thing that comes to my mind is his great love for people. During my childhood, he was the village's "Santa Claus." At Christmas, he bought enough bread to satisfy the whole extended family. He and his wife always invited us to celebrate Christmas with them. We drank tea and ate bread. This invitation was crucial to us because if we missed tea and bread at Christmas, then we would have to wait for the next Christmas. Although my aunt didn't have sufficient teacups, we improvised with plates. Life was difficult for everyone, but my uncle made sure that, at least, at Christmas, we enjoyed what other kids were enjoying. I know that it was a sacrifice for him to be able to do so because he already had a big family of his own. As I reflect on his sacrifices now, I feel ashamed of myself, particularly the way I fail to care for others. At Christmas, he also bought the latest music albums so that the kids would be kept busy, dancing. Not many of us were talented dancers like my cousin Felix and friend Innocent were. But, since it wasn't a dancing contest, we danced to enjoy ourselves and not to win any awards.

In those years, we eagerly waited for Christmas, every year. I was illiterate and didn't know when and how Christmas would come, but I knew that it always would. We had to be patient, and it never failed us. Yes, it always came, and Uncle Chevurombo never let us down. I can imagine what sort of Christmas we would have had if he hadn't invited us to celebrate with his family. Although we always had enough food, my mother couldn't afford to buy even a loaf of bread and a packet of sugar at Christmas. It's not that having bread was ordinary during that time, but most people afforded a few loaves once a year—at Christmas. If there is anything that I learned from Uncle Chovurombo and his wife, it is the power of generosity, love, and working hard. However, it's not easy to reach half the man Uncle Chovurombo is.

My uncle wasn't perfect, and at times we had our differences, but his love always triumphed. He is a workaholic, and he demands more than hard work from everyone under his roof. I say this not because he finds me wanting in that respect, but because I realize that there is always a limit to what a person can accomplish at a particular time. I also know that the human body needs to rest for it to regain the energy it needs to do work. My uncle doesn't think that rest is necessary.

As if that's not bad enough, he is a proud man, and always brags about him being a self-made man, which he is. I think that there is nothing wrong in reminding others, once in a while, of the great things that you have accomplished, but my uncle has the proclivity to overdo it. That pride blinds him from seeing and appreciating how other people try their best, and sometimes fail to reach his standards. He compares his harvest with his neighbors, and most of the time, he finds them wanting. He sometimes thinks that all other occupations are useless except farming, and encourages his sons to leave their town jobs to join him at the farm. He decries the television people who waste their time dancing instead of working on the field.

I had the honor of living with his family for several years. Both his wife and he were very kind and generous to me. He and his wife taught me how to work hard and think wisely. I learned how to milk, yoke, herd cattle, and perform other manly jobs such as building and thatching huts. As I have already mentioned, Uncle Chovurombo believed in hard labor. I don't recall any other family in the village that worked as hard as his.

He was generous too. Occasionally, he would buy us nice clothes. I will never forget the kids' overalls that he bought for his two older sons and me. Mine was blue, and theirs were green. The overalls had the badge "shell" inscribed in yellow on their chest pockets. We became favorite boys of the village girls for a long time because of those clothes. Our childhood lovers would write letters to us using charcoal and cardboard boxes, and we would respond using the same. We were all illiterate, but we could decipher the meanings of whatever was written, or drawn on those boxes. They were love letters, which no one else could read or understand, except us. They were perfect love letters because each recipient could read and understand them the way he or she wanted. That's what love does. It enables the beloved to get deeper meanings and feelings where others don't see or feel anything.

I have already mentioned that I lived with my uncle and aunt and their family for several years. I have already said that we farmed corn and other crops, and harvested surplus food. Enough food was cooked, but the boys were always hungry. Our appetites were insatiable. For us, eating time was madness time. It was survival of the shrewdest. We seemed to live for nothing else except eating. When I look back at that time, I feel ashamed of the eating gimmicks I had to put in place to survive. All boys shared food on the same plate. There was one plate of *sadza* (a thick porridge made from corn meal), and another plate of vegetables or meat that the boys had to share. We were five boys. The girls also shared *sadza* and vegetables, but they were not as voracious as the boys.

Eating time demanded the survival of the fittest. One had to be fast, skillful, and ruthless. Whatever amount of food that was allocated to us, we would finish it in a few minutes. After devouring our share of food, we would then wait for my uncle and aunt to offer us some more. The girls also did offer us some of their food on many occasions. It seemed that the more food we were provided, the hungrier we became. As we played, worked, or herded cows during the day, we would be devising new tactics of out-maneuvering each other in the eating race. I don't think I ever perfected my eating skills like some of my uncles did, for I felt like an amateur during every meal. This feeling may be mutual because they may think that I was the most voracious, a possibility that I don't deny. One of my challenges was that I couldn't swallow hot food, and I wasted time in blowing it with my breath to make it cooler. Of course, there is no doubt that I occasionally climbed to the top of our eating charts. But, of course, everyone survived.

My uncle was an ethical and responsible man who managed to send all his children to school. Although he didn't have enough money to send them to boarding schools, he managed to rent a house in a small mining town where his children could attend a good school, the only high school in Nyajena that enjoyed sponsorship from Rio Tinto, Zimbabwe. It helped quite a great deal because all his sons improved academically. In fact, all of them became academic giants that I always suspected them to be. However, he wasn't lucky with the girls, who continued to struggle academically despite being prayerful and wise ladies. Although they didn't pass their final high school public examinations, they attained wisdom from their studies. That acquisition of practical wisdom is exhibited by the way they provide and care for their families, and the love they have for their friends, family members, and God. On several occasions, I stayed in their rented apartments in Harare and received their care. So I wasn't only cared for by Uncle Chovurombo, but also his children.

My uncle is still alive working as hard as before, but his health is failing. First, it was one of his eyes, and now they say it's his heart. It's sad to note that his most significant gift is also his worst shortcoming. He works so hard and demands hard work from all his children and relatives. If you are not prepared to work harder than your usual best, then you better stay away from him. I don't think that any one of his children would want to subject herself or himself to that hard labor again, particularly now when they do have their own homes, families, means of livelihood. Although hard manual work pays, at times it adversely affects one's health. I know that at some point, Uncle Chovurombo has to come to terms with his age and begin to scale down his physical activities. However, I still don't know how he can be persuaded to do that, but sooner or later something has got to give.

Childhood Health Issues

I had childhood health challenges that were never realized as problematic by my mother and relatives because they weren't serious. My mother, just like other villagers, lacked the knowledge that my ailments were medical conditions that needed medical attention. First, I fainted on multiple occasions for no apparent reason. The first episode that I recall happened when my mother and my siblings were riding a bus going to Mashaba Mine where my father worked. I was three or four years old. I just blacked out. I remember seeing my mother shouting for help, and many other passengers crowding over me. I heard someone yelling, "Open the windows!" Soon, I regained my consciousness, and everything became normal. The episode could have lasted for only a minute or even less. I can't recall any other fainting attack as a toddler, but I have a feeling that quite a few happened.

The other fainting episode that I recall happened when I was about nine. We were doing general work at school, and I felt it coming. I lay on the ground before I blacked out. When I regained my consciousness, I was sweating profusely, and the teacher in charge of general work was kneeling beside me trying to revive me. That episode was a blessing in disguise. It saved me from the meaningless hard labor the students were subjected to at Chitakai Primary School, and perhaps at many other rural schools of that time. The Ministry of Education had christened the program, "Education with Production," which some male teachers had mistaken for "Education with Reproduction" because of their scramble for older female students. They knew it was unprofessional to propose love to school children, but they still had the spirit of the Liberation War in which all laws could be broken without consequences. It wasn't entirely their fault because some of the older girls, who had been Liberation War collaborators (chimbwidos) also seemed to enjoy the game. For some of them, it was priceless to fall in love with a teacher. Indeed, some of them got married to those teachers and raised lovely families.

Anyway, back to how my fainting rescued me from the hard labor at the school. So, whenever it was general work time, I claimed that if I worked in the sun, I would faint, which was to some extent not right, although I believed it to be. The teacher who had witnessed my fainting episode was my witness. I think my passing out had scared him very much that he always sided with me. I say that it wasn't true because I worked in the scorching sun at home all the time, and I never fainted. My fainting wasn't a sickness, for it lasted only about a minute or less, and I would gain full consciousness and use of my body immediately.

The other time I blacked out, I was standing in a queue at the Post Office at Renco Mine. I felt it coming, and I sat down. I blacked out, and when I regained my consciousness, I was sweating. My cousin, who was standing with me was scared. After that, the fainting happened a few more times, with the last attack when I was in Gweru. Sometimes, I could go for five years without experiencing any attacks. Then a miracle happened. I devised my own remedy. Whenever I felt the fainting coming, I would take deep breathes, and that spared me. I haven't fainted in decades. It's no longer a health issue for me.

The second health issue that I have experienced as long as I can remember is abdominal pain, which I later discovered was caused by excessive acids in my stomach. As a kid, I had that sharp pain in my abdomen, almost every day. The pain would just come and go as it pleased. Since this wasn't some severe sickness, no medical attention was sought for me. In fact, during that time, going to the hospital was, in most cases, reserved for severe ailments. The herbs that I usually took during such attacks were initially helpful but eventually lost their efficacy. I had to learn to live with the pain.

I later devised ways of soothing the pain. At first, lying down on my stomach did the trick. I remember spending many nights lying on my belly because any shift from that position caused lots of stomach pain. At some point, this therapeutic gimmick stopped working, and I came up with another. I would sleep on my back on the floor with my knees folded and raised, and my feet on a stool or chair. Where there were no chairs, I would use the wall of the house, and still getting the same results. My feet would fall to the floor after falling asleep. This therapeutic posture was a big pain reliever for me. I also discovered that sipping some cold water when the pain started alleviated the discomfort. Sooner, I found out that drinking too much water brought its fair share of challenges—bedwetting. Those who grew up during my time would know how embarrassing, dehumanizing, and shameful bedwetting was.

I had no solution to the heartburn that I experienced almost every day. At the time, I didn't know that it was called heartburn. I explained to my mother what I felt, and she wouldn't understand my explanation, or she did, but just didn't believe me. I told her that whenever we were weeding in the field, I felt that there was some frying happening in my chest and tummy. It felt like the devil was frying my heart. I hoped to be exempted from working in the fields, but it didn't happen. In the end, my family thought that it was just laziness. Sometimes, I could feel the bitterness of the stomach acids in my mouth as we worked all day long in the fields. Of course, I didn't know that what tasted bitter in my mouth were stomach acids. Sooner, I got to know that whenever I ate some vegetables such as *muboora* (pumpkin leaves), the heart frying would be worse the following day.

Then the War of Liberation (1966–80) came. One of the freedom fighters, whose war name was Tendai Chimurenga gave me some medicines, which almost cured my stomach acids. This is what happened. Every group of freedom fighters had a Medic and Comrade. Tendai was one of those. Many ailing villagers flocked to the base (meeting place) to receive free medications from the freedom fighter. Like other infirm villagers, I also sought help from them. I was about six. Comrade. Tendai gave me about ten packets of *Eno*, which was a powdery stomach acid neutralizer. I didn't know what it was until later in life because I was illiterate at that time. Whenever I felt some discomfort in my stomach, I would put a little bit of the therapeutic powder in a cup, mixed it with water, and drank the mixture. It worked. The pain would go away immediately. I don't remember when I finished the last packet, but the frequency of the stomach pain widened. I was almost healed.

I never had stomach pain throughout my high school and seminary. It was not until 1994, when I was at Wadzanai Training Center, in Harare, when the same stomach pain came back, this time with a vengeance. Sr. Perpetua Lonergan, PBVM, who was the Director of the college at that time, took me to a doctor, who told me for the first time that my stomach discomfort was caused by excessive stomach acids. She prescribed some tablets that I only knew as MMT, and they did wonders whenever I took them. For the following many years, they became almost my daily bread. At some point, I had a barium swallow test to check if I had stomach ulcers, but I didn't. Now, I am in San Antonio, Texas, and the stomach discomfort has increased. I have received education on how to avoid eating food that causes a surge in stomach acids. The physician told me that it was acid reflux or something like that.

My third childhood ailment is what I came to know as an allergy in 1994. From as long as I remember, I had a stuffed nose. Every day, my nose would be congested. I sometimes sneezed continuously. For my mother and grandmother, I was suffering from influenza that could be cured by taking a few doses of *zimbani*, but it never did. *Zimbani* is a popular Zimbabwean herb that is believed to cure colds and influenza. I would try to clear my blocked nostrils, by all means, necessary, but the attempts were futile. Most of the time, blowing out didn't work for me. In fact, it worsened the situation. Usually, blowing in, worked better, but it drove my grandmother hysterical. She didn't like the sound of it, and she would call me a "donkey" whenever I did it. I don't know why she thought that I did it on purpose. I didn't like doing it, but I still did it, again and again, until she went into a frenzy of rage. I didn't want to make my grandmother angry because I loved her, and I think she also liked me. She just didn't understand the discomfort that I was going through.

"Pagara, I don't want you to swallow your mucus. Blow it out," she would say in a rage.

"Yes, grandma," I would respond.

"Why do you do it? Are you hungry? Don't I give you enough food?"

"I am not hungry, grandma. My nose is blocked again. I can't breathe, grandma."

"If you can't breathe, blow it out, not in." She would retort. I wouldn't answer. I would just look at her with my mouth wide open. She never understood why I blew in instead of out. Blowing out never worked for me. Blowing in gave me the temporary relief that I desperately needed. I started hating myself for doing it. All my siblings and cousins never had blocked nostrils, and never blew in mucus. It was only me whose nose was always stuffed. I later devised a breathing method. Whenever my nostrils were blocked, and my grandma was around, I used my mouth to breath. It worked wonders except that my mouth would become very dry. Consequently, I had to frequently drink some water. Sometimes, my grandma would order me to shut my mouth because she feared that flies would enter.

My dry mouth and frequent water drinking heralded another challenge—bedwetting. Although my mother never chastised me for blowing in mucus, bed wetting drove her crazy, and I did it almost every day. I did it not only once, but at times, twice within a single night. I hated doing it, but it just happened. Sometimes it came as a dream only to discover that I had done it again, in my blankets. Wetting my blankets was shameful. If you have never soaked your blankets, you may not have an idea about the embarrassment and shame that accompanies it. It's even more dehumanizing when you are the only one who wets his blankets, and your age mates and juniors don't. Everyone, including the dogs, shamed me. Everybody convinced me that it was my fault that I wetted my bed. I was relieved when the bedwetting stopped. Yes, it did end at some point. Some things don't last forever. I don't know how, but it ended. Every morning I would inspect my blanket and under the reed mate on which I slept, and it was dry. The absence of dampness was a cause for celebration. It meant that there wouldn't be any scolding and shaming from peers and siblings. I regained my dignity.

My allergies just disappeared, and I don't know how and when. I just remember that I had no stuffed nostrils when I was in high school. Then, in 1994, all hell broke loose. The nose stuffing came back with a vengeance. It started like overstayed influenza; then it lingered on. At first, I didn't associate it with my childhood nose stuffing. Later, I discovered that at night, not both nostrils would be blocked. The one on the side of the pillow would be stuffed, and the other one would be clear. Again, the bigger than life, Sister Perpetua Lonergan took me to the physician who declared that I had an allergy, which was incurable. She prescribed some nasal sprays that worsened the blockage and sneezing.

Allergies became my scourge for almost six years. I discovered a few things about my allergy. It only attacked me during winter, and whenever I was in Harare. So, when I went to teach and live in Hurungwe, the allergy disappeared. The allergy didn't attack me in Chicago, so it wasn't about the cold weather. However, it came back when I came to San Antonio, Texas. Some things never change. I have learned to live with it. I take all sorts of relief medications, but I still have it.

I have come to realize that the stomach acids, and nose stuffing and sneezing are somehow connected. I have a fourth ailment, which is a slight headache, which my physician believes is caused by my inflamed sinus. Apart from the headaches, I have lived with my illnesses all my life, and I have learned to function in their presence. I love Texas; it reminds me of my childhood struggles. It feels like one of my great, great grandparents lived here.

CHAPTER 3

John Chitakure

THE WAR OF LIBERATION AND THE STRUGGLE FOR LITERACY

I don't have a clear recollection of when and how the Second Chimurenga (Second Revolution) started, but it did start when the right time had arrived. I don't recall all the details surrounding its beginning because I was too young to remember. In fact, I was illiterate throughout the War, and my time reckoning revolved around Christmas. Historians and eyewitnesses tell us that it started around 1966, and I have no reason to doubt their timeline. Although I don't know the exact dates of the beginning of the War, I know that it ended in 1980 because that's the year I started school. The Second Chimurenga was a revolution, and just like other revolutionary winds, it couldn't be aborted prematurely. It's the struggle that brought about the independence of Zimbabwe. The fight was between the indigenous people of Zimbabwe and the Rhodesian government (Whites) under the leadership of Ian Douglas Smith.

Zimbabwe was a colony of Great Britain for almost a century. The British and their friends had arrived in Zimbabwe, which they named Rhodesia, in 1890, and had declared the country their own property using a fraudulent Concession (The Rudd Concession) that they had obtained from King Lobengula, through hook and crook. When they failed to locate the anticipated gold deposits, they turned to farming. As their population and need for arable land increased, they continued to confiscate land from the indigenous people, who they pushed to areas that weren't suitable for farming. They established many segregative, exploitive, and oppressive laws to the resentment of the indigenous people, who attempted to revolt to no avail. The Ndebele people revolted twice, in 1893 and 1896, and were massacred by the superior and lethal weapon of the white man, on both occasions. The Shona also rebelled in what historians have dubbed, the First Chimurenga of 1896, and were subdued just like the Ndebele. For many years, the indigenous people of Zimbabwe suffered under the exploitive and oppressive rule of the British, until they decided to wage a guerrilla warfare that brought about the independence of Zimbabwe in 1980. During the armed struggle, both sides had myriads of sympathizers, some of whom provided them with arms, intelligence, and human power. The Rhodesians had the West and South Africa, and the nationalists had China, Russia, Mozambique, Zambia, Tanzania, and many other countries, which supported them.

Yes, Christmas was significant to most children in my village because of several reasons. First, it was the most important and enduring of the few notable festivals that we celebrated. Christmas never failed us. It always came at the appropriate time—never too early or too late. The years always seemed longer, but Christmas, like a caring mother, never let us down. During that era, Christmas was so central that events were chronicled as having happened before or after Christmas. Ages were calculated as the total number of Christmases one would have celebrated.

Second, those kids who were lucky enough got new clothes at Christmas. If the clothes were bought a couple of months before Christmas, the fortunate kids had to wait until Christmas to wear them. Friends would give the lucky child congratulatory pinches called *matsvani* to celebrate his new clothes. Third, in most rural villages special food such as rice and bread were eaten only at Christmas, and we didn't seem to ever have enough of the duo. Finally, on Christmas Day, adults would take charge of livestock while we went to the Township to play with our friends. If we were lucky, we would drink sodas at the Township. Not every one of us had the money to buy the drinks, but those who could afford to purchase a bottle of coca cola would allow every member of the cohort to take a sip. It was like the present-day Christians lining to receive the holy blood of Jesus Christ. Of course, in our case, the buyer of the treasured drink acted like the priest. That was the communal spirit that resided in the villages during that time.

We were waiting for the arrival of yet another Christmas when the War of Liberation broke out. Of course, we weren't taken by surprise because we knew that it was on its way. There had been rumors and reports of the brutal War that had already started in some provinces of Zimbabwe, but the people of Machimbira's village didn't expect it to arrive as soon as it did. Again, they didn't imagine that it would be as brutal as it turned out to be. The day the War actually came to our village, it seemed like a joke. It was on one of the winter mornings when the freedom fighters arrived in our village. It was early in the morning, before sunrise. They gathered everyone at a place called KwaVaMumera, on the foot of the Chitakai Mountain. All the villagers, including kids, were obliged to attend the meeting.

I can't remember how many freedom fighters were present at that inaugural gathering, but it was a significant number. Perhaps, there were ten or more freedom fighters. It wasn't easy to count them because we were told that some of them, though present, were invisible. All of them, of course, the visible ones, were armed to the tooth. They had all sorts of guns, namely, bazookas, light machine guns (LMG), sub-machine guns, mortars (*morotero*), among others. Although I had seen guns in the movies that we used to watch at Mashaba Mine, I had never seen live firearms. That was my first day seeing guns at close range. It was abundantly clear that the freedom fighters meant business. They wouldn't carry such lethal weapons if they didn't intend to use them.

Throughout the meeting, the freedom fighters were very friendly and polite. They called all women and men "mother" or "father" respectively. They started teaching people the slogans of the War, and soon everybody seemed to have grasped them. They also taught people how to sing simple war choruses. Most of the tunes were derived from church hymnal tunes, which had been given new words, extolling the Liberation War and its leaders. Somebody brought a radio, and soon the meeting became like another Christmas or dancing party. The fighters seized the day by introducing a new type of dancing that had never been seen by our people before. They called it *Kongonya* Dance, which was accompanied by Kanindo, a music genre that originated from Tanzania and Kenya. This dancing could have misled the villagers into thinking that the War was about dancing and singing. Later, we discovered that the armed struggle was also about death and suffering, not only dancing.

"We are the sons of the soil. We are the revived bones of Ambuya Nehanda. We have been sent to liberate you from the White man's oppression. We will fight the White man and defeat him. We will chase him back to where he came from. When we get our independence, we will be able to walk freely along First Street, in Salisbury. We will drink the White man's beer. White women will come to stay in the rural villages. They will carry buckets of maize on their heads going to the grinding mill. They will fetch water from the rivers using buckets. We will take over their houses and land. But, we can only defeat them if we fight together." This explanation made the slogan, "*Iwe neni tine basa,*" (You and I have a job to do), more significant.

"We need your support. You are the water, and we are the fish. You have to play your part. You, the *povo* will provide us with food and blankets. Your young men will give us the intelligence that we need. The young boys are the *mujibhas* (collaborators). You girls, you will entertain us and wash our clothes. You are the *chimbwidos*. Does anyone of you have a question?" He stopped talking and looked straight into the eyes of the people. Immediately one of the elders' hand went up. The freedom fighter acknowledged him. The elder cleared his voice and spoke.

"Do you think that you will be able to defeat the White man? Don't you know that all of us will rot in jails? The White man is ruthless. Do you want to get all of us killed?" Before he finished talking, the freedom fighter interjected him. He seemed upset. He told him that the War was for everyone, not only the freedom fighters.

Those who didn't want to actively participate in the struggle would be disciplined. He also warned people not to share with anyone what they had heard and seen that day. If the Rhodesian soldiers were to ask about their whereabouts, everyone was supposed to tell them that he had never seen the freedom fighters. Anybody who divulged the information about them would be considered a traitor and would be severely punished.

"If you betray us, we will cut your lips and ears," warned one of the freedom fighters. "We get rid of traitors," he continued. They also warned the witches. "You mothers, you will prepare food for us. Your daughters will bring the food to the *base* (meeting place) for us to consume. If anyone of you tries to bewitch us, we will get rid of her. We have the power to identify witches." They emphasized that they would get rid of witches and traitors in the most brutal way. Although they sounded jovial and friendly, they appeared to be very strict. The meeting ended with more singing and dancing. At long last, the War had started, or it had come to our village.

At first, everything seemed perfect. The freedom fighters had brought entertainment to the village. The villagers respected the comrades or *vana mukoma* (brothers), as they were known. It's difficult to tell if the respect was out of love, or fear, or both. In the beginning, everybody willingly brought food and blankets to the *base* (meeting place). Everybody was so eager to play a part in the revolution. There was no fear of the Rhodesian soldiers because the comrades had assured people of their protection. They told the villagers that they were immortal, and the Rhodesian soldiers' bullets wouldn't harm them. Almost everyone in our village believed them. If there were any skeptics among the villagers, they might have figured out that it wasn't a favorable time for philosophical arguments. For the rest of us, it was a great relief to learn of their immortality. We were so proud to be associated with the invincible and larger than life, freedom fighters.

They also told us that they had been "cooked" in big pots full of magical waters in Mozambique where they were trained. That therapeutic water had enabled them to be invisible whenever they chose. Since they were the sons of the soil or ancestors, they were sacred. Ordinary *povo* (people) weren't allowed to touch them because it would desecrate them. They greeted people using sticks.

Sooner more radios were brought to the *base* (meeting place), and kanindo music was played. The freedom fighters were great dancers and singers. Eventually, most young people learned their type of dance and the *base* became a place of fantastic entertainment. They also brought medicines. In every group of freedom fighters, there was a medic. All the ailing villagers flocked to the *base* to get medication. The *base* became everything—a mini-clinic, a classroom where civic education took place, a point of entertainment, a court where wayward villagers were disciplined, and a partying place where delicious food was served. For most young people, it was easy to fall in love with the *base*.

Although everything was going well, *vana mukoma* kept reminding people that War was brutal. They instructed the *povo* on how to act in the event of an attack by the Rhodesian forces. It was difficult for the people to understand the horrors of War without first experiencing them. But, then one day something went terribly wrong. The freedom fighters had arrived in the village early in the morning, and they were enjoying themselves at the Svimborume *base* with the *chimbwidos* and *mijibhas*. We were busy herding goats and playing in a nearby bush. What we heard first was a deafening explosion that came from the top of the Chitakai Mountain. We made joyful noises, thinking that the freedom fighters had fired the bazooka to signify the beginning of some severe fighting. We were wrong, for the big bang was a signal intended for the Rhodesia forces' jet fighters, which were on their way to our village. Our celebration was to be short-lived.

Suddenly, as if from nowhere, two colossal jet fighters appeared just above us. They were very close to the ground, just above the trees. The noise that followed behind them was nerve-racking and deafening. We had seen airplanes before, but not as aggressive and close to the ground as those jumbo jet fighters. The only aircraft that the villagers had known was Gadzamurivo, whose daily passing through our village, signified the time to begin preparing supper. It was a friendly plane that we could hardly see because of its high altitude. Whenever we saw Gadzamuriwo, we would sing a beautiful song to remind our mothers and sisters that it was about time to begin the preparations for supper. The jet fighters were fearsome. They turned and went over the Svimborume *base* where the freedom fighters were encamped. They turned on and off some light signals, and before we could think of what to do next, all hell broke loose. The jets flew over the *base* for the second time and dropped a barrage of artillery. We started running going back to our homes leaving our livestock scattered. We could see the fire burning above the trees at the *base*, and thick black smoke going up in the sky.

That marked the first encounter between the freedom fighters and the Rhodesian forces that the people of Machimbira's village experienced. No freedom fighter was killed in that clash, but three girls from our village lost their lives. My cousin, Perekai was murdered on that fateful day by a helicopter machine gunner. The helicopter bombed my aunt's (*maiguru*) round hut in which many of the children who had run away from herding goats had sought refuge. When the roof of the kitchen caught fire, most of the children hid under the granary. But, Perekai was unlucky. She tried to run across the road, up the small hill that was about fifty meters behind my aunt's home. She didn't make it. The vampirish shooter from the chopper blew her head to pieces. She died on the sport. She was in her early teens. The lack of freedom fighter fatalities in that battle further reinforced the myth that they were immortal.

The Svimborume encounter changed the *povo's* understanding of the War. The people became aware that the armed struggle was more than just singing, answering to slogans, eating *voetkoeks*, pronounced *fatcooks* (Afrikaner fried dough bread), and dancing. It involved the shedding of blood, not just the blood of the combatants, but also of unarmed civilians. The *povo* became fearful of the War, and they started doubting the proclaimed immortality of the freedom fighters, and the efficacy of their weapons. Although *vana mukoma* had a gun that they called "anti-air," they seemed not to have used it during the attack. They hadn't managed to shoot down the jet fighters and helicopters that hovered very close to the ground. Some of the *mujibhas* and *chimbwidos* who were present at the Svimborume *base* told us that the comrades never tried to shoot down the jet fighters. Instead, they elusively ran away. Later, during the war, we came to know that when the comrades claimed that they could vanish into thin air, what they meant was that they could skillfully evade the enemy.

Another bitter aftermath and disappointment of the Svimborume battle was the freedom fighters' failure to protect the people from the harassment that followed. The villagers who had failed to escape from the village on the day of the attack were later arrested and taken to Renco Mine where they were questioned and released without charges. The comrades also became more aggressive towards the villagers. They accused some villagers of having sold them out to the Rhodesian soldiers. The so-called traitors were brutally killed. No one knows if the accused people were guilty or not. There was no way to tell because there were no proper trials. The freedom fighters were both the judges and executioners.

The comrades also embarked on an unprecedented witch hunt. Anyone who was accused of being a witch was eliminated. The Shona people of Zimbabwe believe that a witch is an evil person who employs evil, secret, and mysterious ways to harm others. Witches are believed to work in cohorts at night and engage in nocturnal orgies at which they devour human flesh, which they would have dug out of graves. Since there was no foolproof way of vetting the accused people, many innocent people perished. There was nothing that resembled a trial. Once you were indicted, your sentence was already predetermined. Sooner, the butchering of the so-called witches and traitors became a form of entertainment. The *povo* seemed to enjoy it. Some of the accused people escaped the ordeal with some savage beatings. Very few were forgiven if they confessed that they were witches, and were willing to stop the evil practices. In our village, far more people were killed by the freedom fighters than by the Rhodesian government forces. The revolution devoured more of its own people than the enemy.

As more encounters between the government soldiers and the freedom fighters were experienced, the *povo* became more fearful of the War. Most of them reluctantly participated in all night vigils (*pungwes*). They feared that they could be attacked by the Rhodesian forces, and the comrades wouldn't protect them. They also feared being accused of some fictitious wrongdoing by the freedom fighters. In addition to that, the people started running out of resources such as chicken. But, the freedom fighters wouldn't take that as an excuse to not bringing food to the *base*. The women had to carry the food on their backs to disguise it as babies. Because of that reluctance, the freedom fighters lost their trust of the people. The women were required to taste the food that they brought to the *base* for poison, for it was claimed that a few freedom fighters had been poisoned by the villagers elsewhere. Most of such accusations were baseless because the freedom fighters didn't have medical equipment and the expertise to diagnose sickness. Any kind of diarrhea would be diagnosed as a result of poisoning.

The Revolution dragged on contrary to the belief that it would be swiftly won. As more people perished, the initial euphoria died out as well. The people got tired of the War. The harassment from both the Rhodesian forces and comrades intensified. As if that didn't cause enough disillusionment, the villagers discovered that the freedom fighters were also mortal. The myth of their immortality was demystified and debunked at Mavuka's village, where six freedom fighters were killed by the Rhodesian soldiers. At that point, it was too late for the villagers to give up their support of the fighters. The red line had been crossed, and there was no going back.

Everyone had to play a part. The women prepared food and perilously carried it on their backs to the *base*. The *chimbwidos* entertained the freedom fighters and washed their clothes. The *mujibhas* had enormous responsibilities. They had to patrol the locality to check for the presence of the enemy soldiers. Once they saw them, there were several things that they had to take note of. First, the number of the soldiers spotted was crucial. The comrades' first question would be, "How soldiers did you see?" Second, the presence or absence of white soldiers had to be taken note of. The white soldiers were feared most because most of them were snipers. Third, the presence or absence of a walkie-talkie was another crucial piece of intelligence. Walk-talkies were used by the Rhodesian forces to request for reinforcement from their superiors. Finally, the presence or absence of NATO, which was a machine gun that was reputed for wreaking havoc in attacks by the Rhodesian soldiers, was supposed to be reported. If any of the above were said to be present, then the comrades would just disappear.

The married men helped the fighters to carry their caches, and by providing intelligence. We, the children were responsible for spreading the news of the arrival of the comrades. One day, we nearly got into trouble because of our overzealousness. I was heading cattle with two of my childhood friends. We met the comrades in a small bush that was closer to our homes. They sent us to tell the women to bring the food to the *base*. They also instructed us that the children weren't allowed to attend the *base* meeting because it had become too dangerous. We made a mistake. We changed the message. We told the villagers that everyone, including children, was required to attend the meeting. We changed the invitation message because we also wanted to participate in the gathering. We didn't want to miss the delicious food, particularly the *voetkoeks* that were served at the *base*. The comrades were enraged to see both adults and children coming to the station. We were reprimanded and commanded not to do it again. But, only after we had had our delicious meal.

The End of the War

That was the Second War of Liberation. It went on and on until the initial euphoria died out. The people became weary and fearful. Most of their chickens were gone, and the freedom fighters continued to refuse to eat green vegetables, especially okra. But, before it was too late, the War ended. Nothing goes on forever. There were elections after which we were told that Comrade (Cde.) Robert Mugabe had won. At long last, we had our independence in 1980. The people rejoiced. There were huge parties that were thrown to celebrate the victory.

But, there were surprises too. The whites were still living in towns and still owned their homes. They even owned the land, which was one of the most critical grievances that had caused the revolution. Some of them became ministers and high-ranking officials in the new government of Mr. Mugabe. To the worst horror of most people, Mr. Ian Douglas Smith, the last Rhodesian Prime Minister, wasn't arrested and made accountable for the innocent lives that he had taken. As if that wasn't treacherous enough, the Whites still owned the means of production. Some of the former Rhodesian government soldiers were incorporated into the new Zimbabwe National Army. It dawned on the *povo* that the comrades hadn't been very truthful with them. Many people felt betrayed. It was like the people who had perished in Zimbabwe and in other countries had sacrificed their lives in vain. Songs had been composed in memory of thousands of Zimbabweans who had died at the hands of the Rhodesian forces at both Nyadzonya and Chimoio, in Mozambique. To imagine that their deaths would never be avenged was unfathomable.

We were later told that Cde. Robert Mugabe, who had become the new Prime Minister of independent Zimbabwe had forgiven all the perpetrators of their war crimes. He had told the people who witnessed his inauguration rally in Salisbury (Harare) that the people of Zimbabwe could no longer resist the bonds of love that bound them together. Zimbabweans, irrespective of their color, race, and gender had become one family. At first, we couldn't understand how one person could forgive on behalf of all Zimbabweans, dead and alive. We couldn't understand why the Prime Minister had to impose reconciliation upon the people that had never asked for it, and perhaps never appreciated it. No reparations were paid for the suffering the indigenous people had endured at the hands of the colonizers for almost a hundred years. Reconciliation without compensation was very unAfrican. Those whites who were thinking of emigrating from Zimbabwe to other countries decided to stay. Some of those who had already left the country came back. Overnight, our Prime Minister became the blue-eyed guy of the West. He had put to rest the rumors that said that he would make independent Zimbabwe, a Communist country. Later, we learned about the benefits of the reconciliation that the Prime Minister had offered to the perpetrators of the war crimes. Even before that, we trusted our Prime Minister, and we believed that he wouldn't mislead us.

Chitakai Primary School, Here I come

Of course, Zimbabwe's independence brought about many positive changes. Some of us, whose formal education had been indefinitely delayed, could now go to school. I was thrilled because I really wanted to learn how to write. Some of the boys who had been to school before the revolution could read and write. I couldn't do both. I very much envied some of my cousins and friends, who could write their names and a few Shona words. Chitakai Primary School opened its doors in May in 1980. The school was just a school in the name because there were no classrooms. The classroom blocks had been destroyed during the War. There were no staff houses. Some teachers had to rent rooms in the villages that were closer to the school. Local teachers operated from their rural homes. The time for destruction was gone, and the time for reconstruction had arrived. In the classrooms, there were no chairs for both teachers and students. Most of the students had no school uniforms. The former *mujibhas* and *chimbwidos* of the Liberation struggle went back to school as well. Everyone wanted to receive an education, which had been a privilege of a few in the colonial era. Everyone wanted to be able to read, write, and perhaps speak the Queen's language. The imperial government had taught the people that the acquisition of formal education could facilitate some social transformation in their lives.

The government provided us with books, pens, and pencils. The headmaster of Chitakai Primary School was Mr. Matake, a charming and big-hearted man. We loved him. He liked singing and teaching us Christian songs. There were songs for the school assembly and songs for dismissal. Some of the earliest teachers were Mr. Mukungwa, popularly known as Chuma, Mr. and Mrs. Zvakasikwa, Mr. Ndebele, Mr. Masese, and many others. The teachers had a big task of transforming the students' mentality from that of war collaborators, into that of students. It wasn't an easy task. Most teachers had to resort to corporal and other unorthodox disciplinary measures. They had to. Otherwise, the school would have become ungovernable.

When the initial euphoria of receiving a free education was passed, some students ran away from school. Some had taken up the habit of smoking and drinking alcoholic drinks, and the school authorities forbade that. A few of the students realized that the indiscipline of the revolution had no place in the school, and left. But, other former *mijibhas* and *chimbwidos* stayed put. Receiving school discipline wasn't easy for some of them, but they persevered.

With the joint efforts of the government, well-wishers, parents, teachers, and students, the school slowly took shape and discipline was restored. Classroom block after block was completed. There were other challenges too. Some students were too old for the First Grade, and they tried to skip it, which proved to be disastrous for them. There were also students who had gone as far as the Third Grade before the War, yet they repeated the First Grade in 1980. Such students were the spoilers because they already knew how to write, and that misled the teachers into thinking that all of us understood what they were teaching. Most of them were appointed group leaders who were responsible for assisting other group members to learn during group discussions. Some of them abused their positions by punishing the students under their supervision. Some teachers didn't permit group leaders to discipline other students, yet remained indifferent if they noticed a group leader punishing other students.

Learning to read and write wasn't as easy as I had anticipated, but I tried my best. At the end of the first term, I came out number six out of over fifty students. I was upset because I had expected to do better. I wanted to be at the top of the class, but I didn't know what I needed to do to improve my performance. Emmanuel Marapira, a classmate, and friend from Mavuka's village came to my aid. I guess he had been to school before the War and knew the gimmicks of getting a good grade. He was brilliant too. He taught me how to prepare for examinations. We studied how to spell words together, and it worked. We completed primary school at Chitakai and went to Mudarikwa Secondary School in 1986. At that time, Emmanuel had become truant and had completely lost his desire for schooling. He had become too busy with the Jack of all Nations Church to which he had converted. That church had been brought to Mavuka's village by a certain Mapipi, a Mozambiquean, who worked as a herdboy at one of the villagers' home. At some point, Emmanuel transferred to a different school. We remained good friends for many years.

I quickly mastered the art of getting good grades by studying at home. Although there wasn't much time to review learning material at home, I used the little time that I had. Consequently, every term I came out number one. My teachers and other students knew that John Tsaurai would always be number one. There was no question about it. Yes, I used Tsaurai as my last name because when I started going

77

to school, I was living with my uncle, Mr. Tsaurai. He is the man whose nickname was Chovurombo. He and his wife treated me just like one of their own sons. He bought school uniforms for me. I used Tsaurai, as my last name until at the beginning of 1985, when I started Grade Seven. I switched to Chitakure at the beginning of Grade Seven because it would be the name on my birth certificate, which I didn't have yet.

At the end of my Fourth Grade, some of my teachers encouraged me to skip Grade Five. I did. I went straight from Grade Four to Grade Six. It worked for me. At the end of the first term of 1984, I came out at the top of about fifty students. This upset some students' academic record, who until then had been on the top of that class. There were many gifted students in that class, but no one ever gave me the type of challenge that would stop me from coming first in my class. It's not that I worked harder than other students, but I was gifted. Many students worked harder than I, but they never improved their grades. As I revised my school work in preparation for a test, I would imagine the sort of questions the teacher would set, and I never went wrong. As I continued to perfect the gimmick, most tests became so predictable, and I would get almost every question correct.

The Class Boycott

The long-awaited Grade Seven came, and our teacher was Mr. Muzinda. He was a hardworking and intelligent teacher, but some students told us that he wasn't as good as Mr. Mbavha, who was teaching the other Grade Seven class. Mr. Muzinda was also gifted in music. He could read music and was the choirmaster of the school choir. I still remember some of the beautiful tunes that he taught us. But that wasn't good enough for some of my classmates. We envied our colleagues who had a different teacher who was reputed for being very intelligent. Our resentment of Mr. Muzinda worsened when he took to the habit of beating us up for no apparent reason. We revolted. All the boys except two rebelled. The girls were too scared of him that they decided to grin and bear his abuses. We refused to go into the classroom. We demanded the expulsion of Mr. Muzinda, who was at the period, a Zimbabwe Integrated Teacher Education Course (ZINTEC) student. He hadn't seen it coming. So when it came, he wasn't expecting anything like that boycott. He was petrified. The strike was led by two of the older boys, who were very influential and persuasive to the rest of us. Most of us were mere followers. The presumably harmless students had gone berserk. Our teacher had not realized that, if you push a dog into a corner, it may become aggressive and bite you.

When the time for a dialogue came, we knew what we wanted and didn't want. We wanted a new teacher, not Mr. Muzinda. Mr. Mashasha, who was the headmaster at that time refused to bow down to our demands. We continued with our strike. We had our lessons from one of the student's English dictionary. We would go to school every day and attend the morning assembly, after which we would disappear into the small hills that were closer to the school. Eventually, we grew tired of the strike and went to report our case to a certain Zimbabwe African National Union, Patriotic Front (ZANU PF) youth leader. We found him at Guwa Township and brought him with us to the school. He sort of chaired our meeting with the headmaster, who tactfully refused to give us a new teacher. We agreed to go back to class on the condition that Mr. Muzinda would stop beating us up. It was an awkward compromise, but we got some benefits out of it.

Yes, we had lost a considerable amount of learning time, yet we settled for something less than our original goal. We didn't get a new teacher—a big disappointment, but we regained our dignity and respect from our teacher. He stopped beating up students and continued working as hard as before. Now, as I reflect on the class boycott, I think that Mr. Muzinda was an excellent teacher. His only mistake was his penchant for beating up students for no apparent reason. Please, don't judge him because, at that time, corporal punishment was legal in Zimbabwe. Most teachers used it. When the Grade Seven examination results came out, all the students who had written it at Chitakai had failed. It was soon discovered that the failure was a result of a computer error. The scripts were regraded, and most students passed with flying colors. For me, that was the beginning of the struggle for education.

My Struggle for Education

We finished our Grade Seven examinations in October of 1985. We were supposed to continue attending classes until December of that year. Mr. Muzinda and the other Grade Seven teacher had already started introducing high school learning material to us. It was exciting to learn that it was possible to subtract two from one, whose answer until then was, "it can't." I felt that all the teachers who had told us that it was impossible to subtract a larger number from a smaller number had misled us. I quickly forgave Mr. Muzinda because he is the teacher who had debunked the myth.

I didn't stay in school until December. I left school at the end of October because I had to find a job. There was nobody in our extended family who was willing or could afford to pay my school fees at the high school the following year. I had two brothers from the other father who were working, but they couldn't assist. I didn't begrudge them for that because they had no obligation to pay my school fees. Also, I didn't quite know them because I had met both of them only once. My uncle, Chovurombo was overwhelmed at that point. He had several children that needed education too. My mother struggled to make ends meet, and she couldn't afford to pay my school fees. I quickly realized that there was nobody who would help me despite my academic brilliance. Like they say, "Graves are full of indispensable men," I knew that if I didn't do something, I would soon be committed to the dustbins of history.

I found a job as a cattle herder a few miles away from home. I worked there from October to December 1985. I got some money, but unfortunately, I didn't use it to pay my school fees. Somebody had told me about a particular school called Ratleshoek in Chipinge, where students could exchange their services for education. The school had vast tea plantations in which students traded their labor for education. I, with two friends, took the bus to Chipinge to look for school places. The trip was doomed. When we arrived at Rattleshoek, we found out that the school had been temporarily closed because students had gone on strike. I think that was at the end of 1985. We didn't see anyone. We came back home to Masvingo empty-handed. We had wasted our hard-earned money.

In December of 1985, we tried again. This time, only Vitalis and I went back to Chipinge. It was another doomed endeavor. Our major setback was optimism. We thought that we wouldn't need bus fare for the return journey because we would get the Form One places that we were looking for. We were very wrong. This trip nearly ended up in utter disaster. We failed to get Form One places that we desperately needed. We weren't prepared for that. We had to go back home, but we had no bus fare to board the bus back to Masvingo. We decided to walk from Ratelshoek Secondary School to Chipinge town. It was a long journey. If we reached Chipinge, only God would know how we would travel from Chipinge to Masvingo. But we were young and full of reckless optimism. On that day, it was raining heavily. Our clothes were soaked in water, and we kept walking. Then a miracle happened. We waved down a big truck driver, and he stopped for us. We briefly explained our predicament, and he waved us in. Within one hour or so, we were in Chipinge, but that wasn't the end of the struggle. We still needed bus fare to travel the 243.5 kilometers from Chipinge to Masvingo.

We had an idea. We looked for a Catholic Church. We were directed to the catechist's residence at one of the government schools in one of the locations. We were tired, hungry, and soaked to the bone. The catechist was Mr. Taguta. He welcomed us, gave us some food, and a place to spend the night. The following day, he convinced the leader of Parish to donate some money for our bus fare. The money we got was only enough to take us to Masvingo, but we still wanted to go to Nyajena, about a hundred kilometers from Masvingo. We had no money, and we knew nobody who could help us in Masvingo.

We decided to walk from Masvingo to Nyajena. It wasn't easy because I had sprained my ankle in Chipinge, and my leg had swollen and painful. Every step that I took made it more painful. Vitalis volunteered to carry my luggage as well as his. He also found a walking stick for me. We were about to reach Morgenster Mission (32 kilometers from Masvingo) when another miracle happened. We heard the sound of a car behind us. As the car approached, we discovered that it was Mr. Matapura's truck. Mr. Matapura was the chairman of our home Parish, St. Teresa's Guwa. His lorry stopped, we jumped in, and within an hour we were home. That journey could have taken us for about two days by foot.

We were so stubborn and unwise. We refused to accept defeat. We went back to Ratleshoek again in January 1986. We arrived at Ratelshoek High School when the term was about to start. There were no places. The head, Mr. Ashley Coopey advised us to go to Ratelshoek Primary School to repeat Grade Seven, which would assure us of Form One vacancies at Ratelshoek Secondary School the following year. We agreed. We started working on the tea estate. It was pure hard work. I had always considered myself a hard worker, but the tea estates proved me wrong. We were placed in work gangs. Mine was Gang Seven. We would wake up early in the morning and run all the way to the tea fields. One needed his *muringo* (measuring stick) and *seketo* (reed basket). We spent about eight hours in the tea estates, every day. Classes were conducted at night. I worked for about three weeks, and then gave up.

At the end of every day, I was so exhausted that I had no strength to attend the night school that we were supposed to participate in. To worsen the matter, students were being ill-treated at the tea estates. Anyone who failed to pluck up a specific weight of tea leaves per day would be beaten up severely by the gang foreman. The day before I ran away from that school, I had witnessed one of the boys being beaten up by the foreman. The beating was so severe that he soiled his shorts. I wasn't learning to pluck tea leaves as fast as I was supposed to, and I received a stern warning from foreman Bhobho. I was told that if I didn't improve my work performance, I would be treated like the other boy the next day. I knew that the foreman meant it. I shivered with fear. That evening, I told Vitalis that I was going back home the following day. He too wanted to come with me, but he didn't tell me. Again, he didn't have bus fare. I could have lent him some money if he had said to me that he too wanted to go back home. He had to wait for the payday that was about a week away. I boarded the bus and left Ratelshoek Primary School before I attended even a single class. I also quit before I got my first salary. I had spent all the money that I had worked for the previous year and got nothing in turn.

Vitalis came home the following week. His trip from Chipinge wasn't without challenges. He had to sell his only jersey to supplement his bus fare. The man who bought it tried to con him. They had a big kerfuffle on the bus. Eventually, he arrived home. I then went to Mudarikwa Secondary School to register for Form One. I had no uniform, no school fees, and no shoes. That was the beginning of 1986. I should have preserved my servings for my school fees instead of pursuing the Rattleshoek winds.

I went to school for about three weeks, but I was sent home almost every day because I hadn't paid school fees. Then, another crazy idea came. The three of us, Hosea, Vitalis, and I decided to try Mukosi Secondary School. We had been told that even those without school fees could attend school there without being sent home all the time. Other students from nearby villages were already attending school there. We stayed at Mukosi until the end of April 1986. Only three weeks after we had been there, the headmaster started sending those students who hadn't paid school fees home.

As I look at it now, I realize that going to Mukosi was not a sound decision. I did what Shona people call *gundamusaira*, which can be translated as following the crowd. As I came to know it later, one of my friends, Hosea Mutinha, had misled us into following him to Mukosi. He had been involved in some mischief of some kind and was disciplined by the headmaster. For him to save face, he decided to transfer to another school. He then misled his young brother, Vitalis and I into believing that we could attend school for free at Mukosi Secondary school. I learned that making decision basing on the instigation of the mob isn't right.

I Became A Cow Herder/Cowboy

Again

I left Mukosi Secondary School and looked for a job. I quickly got one at a nearby Farm, which was situated near Mashate Township. My boss was a young man who worked as a cow deep tank caretaker. That man believed in hard work. I worked like I had never worked before. After a hard work's day in the fields, or filling up the deep tank with water, we would come back home for breakfast. I will always remember how my boss's teacup was so big that it was almost ten times my own cup. I was allowed only one cup of tea. Even if I wanted to have more than one cup of tea, there was no way of doing that because after both of us had filled up our first cups, there was literally nothing left in the big teapot. I worked there for two weeks and decided to quit before I got my first wages, which were later collected by my mother.

I went to Tadzembwa where I got a job as a cattle herder at some home, which was a mile away from Mapakomhere Secondary School. The landlady was a sweet woman who was considered a prophet at the Zion Christian Church that was led by Mrs. Chifaya, also known as *Mai* Zadok. At Mapakomhere, there were many students who I knew from Chitakai School. I also met Jeffrey Madhoyi, a well-known and accomplished Zion Christian Church drummer. I watched him perform, and I felt he was excellent. I started the job in the middle of the either May or June of 1986, and my employer refused to pay me for the two weeks that I worked that month. My first wages came when I had worked for one and half month, but the payment was for one month. She kept telling me that she would give me the money later, but she never did until I left. I visited her a couple of times after I had left her employment, but she still refused to give me my money.

It was when I was at Tadzembwa when a miracle almost happened. My mother came to Tadzembwa bearing excellent news. She had gone to Zivezano Secondary School, which belonged to the father of a certain renowned government minister of Zimbabwe. She told me that the old man had agreed to have me study at Zivezano Secondary School while working for my fees in his fields. My labor would pay my school fees. It seemed that other boys were also working for their school fees at the same school. So, I was supposed to go there and report to this good man as soon as possible. I was ecstatic. I had never been happier in my life.

The following day, I bade my Tadzembwa employer farewell and took the bus from Muchakata Township to Chenhuwe in Majiri. I spent the night at my relatives' place in Madanhire's village. The following day, I went to Zivezano Secondary School and reported to the old man. He came to the gate, empathetically listened to my story, and then told me to go and talk to his daughter, who was a teacher at Shonganiso Primary School, just across the road from the secondary school. I went to her classroom and knocked on the door. She came out and looked at me and grimaced as though she wanted to throw up. I introduced myself and told her about my mother's visit to her place. The good lady told me that she wouldn't talk with me unless I had a haircut. She said to me that my hair was too long and nauseating to her.

I found her command very simple to fulfill. I went back to her father's house, borrowed a pair of scissors, and came back to the high school, where I requested the first student I met to give me a haircut. He agreed, and soon I had a bald head. I went back to the woman who had the powers to either answer my prayers or seal my fate. She smiled when she opened the door of her classroom for the second time that day. I narrated my story, and she listened. I told her about my mother who had talked with her a couple of days ago, and she didn't seem to recall her. I knew at once that this trip was another waste of time. She then told me that she had no place for me because there were too many students who were working for their school fees on her father's farm. I cried all the way back to Madanhire village where I had left my luggage. I had lost a golden opportunity to receive an education. The following day, I was on the bus back to my cow herding job at Tadzembwa. My employer was overjoyed to see me back again. I got my job back, and I worked there until the end of August 1986.

I still don't know why the Shonganiso lady changed the goal posts like that. When she talked with my mother, she had agreed to give me a job in exchange for school fees, but when I spoke with her, she didn't even try to listen to my story. But

I never held that against her. I knew very well that she had the right to either refuse or accept my labor in exchange for an education. I might have failed the interview when I appeared in her classroom with hair that was half a centimeter long. I still don't know why my hair scared her so much. Yes, I felt devastated, but that wasn't the first disappointment that I had encountered in my pursuit to acquire an education. After all, she wasn't related to me and had no obligation to assist me in any way.

I left the Tadzembwa job in August and got another. The agricultural extension worker at Guwa Township, Mr. Masoja, wanted me to herd his cows in Zimuto. I went to Zimuto at the end of 1986. I had two reasons for going to Zimuto. First, although I had worked for about six months, I still hadn't gathered enough money to pay for my school fees at secondary school. I still needed money for my education. Second, Mr. Masoja promised me that he would send me to school the following year. I agreed that he would pay me less money than I had been paid by my other employers so that the money that he withheld would contribute towards my school fees. Mr. Masoja was an honest man, and I trusted him. I admired him because he sounded very educated, erudite, and kind. In November, we went to Zimuto aboard a District Development Fund lorry.

My new employer and his family were very kind to me. He gave me some of his used clothes that he no longer needed. I was overjoyed to know that I would be going back to school the following year. January 1987 came, and I waited eagerly to hear Mr. Masoja's decision about my going back to school. He had told me that I would go to either Mutatiri or Mazambara Secondary School. Although I was a cow herder (*mubhoyi wen'ombe*), it was possible to go to school because the whole village had a cattle herding roster. Each family would take care of the animals for about two days in a month. If I had been allowed to go to school, I would miss only two days of school per month. We agreed that I would work in the fields after school and on weekends. This was a golden opportunity for me to receive an education.

When Mr. Masoja finally came home on one of the weekends, I received another big blow. He told me that he could no longer afford to send me to school. He didn't say the reason, and he had no obligation to give me one. It was another shattered dream. I had spent six months hoping and planning. I started thinking of another plan of getting an education.

Something embarrassing happened at almost the same time. All along, I had been allowed to use the bedroom of Mr. Masoja's daughters. This was possible because the daughters used their parents' bedroom, which they shared with their mother, except for only one weekend in a month when their father was around. On that shameful day, I came back home from fetching firewood and found out that all my blankets and suitcase had been removed from that room and placed in the granary, which was to become my new bedroom until I left. The Masojas had discovered lice in their blankets and had figured out that they had come from me. I think they were right because lice were insects that tormented the poor, who didn't wash their clothes and blankets frequently. The Masojas were rich and clean, and the vampirish insects had no business with them.

I never contested the allegation. Even if I wanted to, I wasn't given an opportunity to do so. Also, if I had been given a chance to challenge the ownership of those shameful insects, I would be too embarrassed to present my argument. In fact, the way they dealt with the issue left me with some dignity. They just removed my belongings from their daughters' bedroom, placed them in the granary, washed their blankets, and told me why they had done so. They never talked about it again. They never laughed at me. It was so humiliating, but I survived it. They helped me escape the excruciating shame by not mentioning it again, at least, in my presence. They continued to treat me with respect after that incident. I learned a lesson or two. I washed my blankets every weekend and managed to get rid of the bugs.

Mr. Masoja then encouraged me to apply to Rapid Results College, which was a correspondence school. The information about the fees was sent to me within two weeks, and I was disappointed when I showed it to Mr. Masoja. He couldn't assist me because it was too expensive. My wages were also not sufficient to pay the fees. I aborted the plan and decided to leave the Masoja job because the money that I was getting was too little. I had agreed to the low wage hoping that I would be sent to school the following year. I didn't hold that against him because he had no obligation to send me to school. I was a mere *mubhoyi wen'ombe*, and during that time, and perhaps even now, most cow herders were vulnerable to exploitation. I didn't think that I was different from other *mabhoyi en'ombe* who toiled for peanuts. I learned not to take people's promises seriously.

Then in April, as I was planning to find another employer to exploit me, I received a letter from Vitalis Mutinha, one of my childhood friends. A local businessman at Guwa Township who was the Parish chairperson of St. Teresa Catholic Church, wanted *mugaisi* (grinding mill operator). It was a good job and was well-paying. I accepted the offer and then gave my notice to the Masojas. A big mistake. I shouldn't have done that. My employer's wife wasn't happy about it. There were reasons for that. I was a hard and diligent worker. I could be trusted with her girls since she had a kraal of them. She didn't want me to go, but I had reached a point of no return. The promised job was lucrative and dignified. It was my only opportunity to get enough money for education. Then she decided to do something that I will never forget. She made sure that I ate *sadza* and vegetables every day. *Sadza* is some thick porridge made from cornmeal and water, which is the staple food in Zimbabwe and many other African countries. So, whenever she cooked some meat, she would give me vegetables only. I became an unwilling vegetarian.

Eating vegetable every day wasn't a big issue for me, but the problem was that we shared the same plate of *sadza* with her children. I had eaten vegetables all my life, and they didn't bother me at all. What bothered me was that they would want me to sit with them as they devoured their meat while I ate *sadza* with vegetables. To worsen the matter, she would send me to Zimuto Mission to buy some broilers. I would slaughter the boilers, but wouldn't eat them. I never asked why she was doing that, but I was later told by a friend that one of her daughters had said that her mother didn't want to waste her delicious meat on a herd boy who had given her notice.

I am writing this not to demonize Mrs. Masoja, who I think was very kind to me. I share this experience to teach the reader a few lessons about how our final treatment of people may overshadow all the good we might have rendered them. You may be very helpful and kind to someone for a long time, but that can quickly be forgotten, if your last treatment of that person leaves a lot to be desired. If Mrs. Masoja weren't a wonderful person right from the beginning of my stay at her home, I wouldn't be complaining about her last treatment of me. I was surprised that such a good person could afford to act like that. I knew of a few *mabhoyi en'ombe* who were treated worse than that. There was the talk of a herd boy who worked for a certain businessman in the same locality, who was forced to wash the underwears of his employer's wife. For readers who know little about African culture, this may not sound wrong at all. But for Zimbabweans, women's underwear is sacred, and it was grossly improper for that woman to ask her male cow herder to do that.

There are several things for which I will ever be grateful to Mr. Masoja. He inspired me to love to read. He taught me to hope for a better future. He encouraged me to be a diligent worker. He told me stories of people in Western literature whose fortunes had changed because of hardworking, honesty, perseverance, and diligence. I took his advice seriously, and I am happy that I did. When I look back at it now, I realize that sometimes good information can change a person's life. Although he broke his promise about sending me to school, he inspired me with his stories. Whenever he came home, he would stop by the nearby township to socialize with his friends at Mudukuti's beer hall. By the time he would arrive home, he would be intoxicated, but never failed to encourage me to read and work hard. I never heard him giving the same advice to his own daughters. I think that he respected me, and saw something within me that he didn't see in his daughters. There were times when I felt that his encouragement was useless because I was already doomed. Now I know that he was right. If he were still alive, I would go back to Mahoto to thank him for his encouragement.

I took Mr. Masoja's counsel seriously. I got some reading material from Luck Mware, who was a student at Mutatiri Secondary School during that time. Richie Masendeke, who was in Form Two at Gokomere High School generously shared his lecture notes with me. He also loaned me his History textbooks. I will never forget him giving me a lecture about the grievances of the First Chimurenga while sitting on the grave of his deceased father. Richie was a good friend. Although he belonged to a middle-class family, he treated me with respect. This was at a time when herd boys were called *makarushu*, a derogatory term used for Mozambiquean refugee herd boys. It's a pity that Richie died young. He is one of the few people who knew that I had educational aspirations, just like other children of my age.

Working as a Grinding Mill Minder and Bartender

When the job notice expired, I went back home to Nyajena and took up my new job. I joined Mr. Matapura's team that was stationed at Chidzidzi, which was a squatter camp. There was another employee who worked at the same place when I arrived. He was a married man and had gained the trust of our employer through his hard work. I loved my new job and considered myself fortunate to have it. The only challenge that I had was that I stayed at the employer's home at Chipumho village. I would walk to and from Chidzidzi every morning. The journey was about seven kilometers. When the grinding mill failed to perform as my employer had hoped, I was transferred to Zengeya Shopping Center where I became a bartender. My employer was a very generous person, but one had to work proficiently. Although he was a hard man to please, he trained me to be a man. One had to be alert all the time. He was the type of man who would severely and publicly reprimand you even for a slight mistake. To meet his standards, one had to work hard. Things had to be done right.

One of the things that I will ever be grateful to this employer was that he forbade me to stay at Chidzidzi with the other employee. The reason? He didn't want me to get involved with women because I was still too young for that. He feared that the other employee would wrongly influence me. The employee was well-known for his promiscuity. There are times when I think that it wasn't this man's fault that he was a womanizer. He wasn't handsome, yet women loved him. He was a shopkeeper in the middle of a squatter camp, and all the loose women tried their luck with him. Most thought that the store belonged to him. Of course, they got something out of their short-term relationship with him. There were days when I arrived at Chidzidzi early in the morning before the man, and his one-night lovers woke up. I would see him offering some of those women a packet of sugar or a bottle of cooking oil for an all night's job. On many occasions, I heard several women challenging him.

"I heard that you like women and you are masterful in bed. I want to challenge you tonight. Are you available?" A woman would inquire.

"At what time do you want to come?" The man would ask while smiling. That's how most of his deals were struck. One day it rained heavily, and all the small rivers were overflowing with water. I had to spend the night at the shop. Just before we had our super, we had a visitor, a very young lady, and I could tell that she was one of the challengers of the shopkeeper. When time to go to bed came, I prepared my bedding in one corner of the store and the shopkeeper with his young challenger in another. The room was of medium size, but there were about four meters that divided our beddings. The duo was respectful enough, for they didn't engage in their sacred games until I was fast asleep. When I eventually woke up in the middle of the night, the holy games were in progress. Soon I went back to bed. I don't know how many times I woke up that night, and every time that I did, the sacred music was on. The youthful contender was indeed up to the contest. Luckily, the room was pitch dark, so I couldn't see them. What I only heard were the sounds and noises. It was like a battle between two elephants. Early in the morning, the woman got a 2kg packet of sugar as a reward for her night's toiling. She heartily thanked the opponent for a game well played, and the prize.

So, my employer was right to say that I was too young to live with such a man. It doesn't mean that I was unprincipled at that time—I was. My employer was a God-fearing man, and he genuinely worried about me. He didn't want me to die of HIV/AIDS, which was at its peak at that time. Although that piece of advice wasn't necessary because I wasn't deficient with regard to sexual morality, I still think that he helped me. He was right. I was too young to die. I had plans for the future. I wanted to go back to school and finish high school.

Back to High School

The other thing that became a blessing in disguise for me while working at Mr. Matapura's place was that I didn't receive my salary every month, but I knew that it was there. All the employees had account books in which the employer entered their wages. If any employee needed to buy something, she would get it from the big store the employer owned and had the amount subtracted from her account. This arrangement might not have worked for other employees, but it did for me. I didn't need cash for anything because the employer provided food for us.

When I decided to go back to school at the end of 1987, the employer was upset. He trusted me and wanted me to continue as his bartender, but I was determined to go back to school. He thought that my going back to school would be a waste of time. I had spent two years out of school, and he believed that the world had already corrupted me, and I was beyond schooling. He had seen that happening to some of his employees and relatives, who had joined his business before they finished primary education and never dreamt of going back to school. He didn't realize that I was different because my only dream at that point was to go back to school. I insisted. When he didn't send a replacement to Zengeya, where I was stationed, I closed the beer hall and went to Guwa Township where he and his family lived, and I was warmly received. It was one of the bravest things that I had ever done. He gave me the money that he owed me. I used some of the cash to buy school uniform. In January 1988, I went back to Mudarikwa Secondary School.

Since I had fallen behind my primary school classmates, I decided to skip Form One and went straight to Form Two to join the group that I had left behind when I jumped Grade Four at Chitakai Primary School. At Mudarikwa, I met new students who had come through Makumbe Primary School and other primary schools. There were the likes of Denford Mapuru, Chiedza Zengeya, Zvandasara Muvungani, Billiam Mahachi, and many others. It really felt good to be back in school. I paid all my fees for that year using the money that I had earned from my last employer. Things looked good.

I completed Form Two in 1988 and passed all the subjects. At the end of Form Two, all my money was gone, and I was back to square one. I applied for a scholarship from the Gweru Diocese Education Fund, through Father Josef Haag who was my Parish Priest. I got partial sponsorship from the Diocesan Education Secretary who at that time was Father Joe Nyika. I augmented the scholarship money by performing some piece works that our headmaster, Mr. Issac Mutamba made available at the school. These piece works were his own way of helping poor students finance their education. One of the jobs was to gather concrete stones for the building of classroom blocks and teachers' houses. The wages earned from such piece works helped me to go through Form Three. It wasn't easy, but my dream to acquire an education was so compelling that nothing could stop it.

I had a pair of shoes that I had bought in 1988, which I guarded jealously. I wanted the shoes to last forever because I had no money to buy another pair. I would put the boots in a plastic bag and carry them in my hand until I was about to arrive at school. There was a small stream that never ran dry, just about half a kilometer from the school in which I would wash my feet, and put on my shoes. As soon as school ended, I would take off my shoes, place them in a plastic bag, and then walked home barefoot. I had to take care of my shoes because the school was far away, and the rocky path to the school was covered with long grass. To worsen the matter, I had to climb up a couple of mountains on my way to and from school. However, despite the excellent care I took of my only pair of shoes, they gave way to age. The heels started coming out. I had to keep them in place using nails. Sometimes those pins would come through the soles of the shoes and would prick my feet. I had to stop from time to time, pick up a stone, and hit the protruding nails from the inside of the shoes. But, that was the way things were. It wasn't only me who had challenges. Other students had their fair share of problems too. I continued to perform well at school. I had to. In fact, I was almost always at the top of the class. But, I could feel the impact of the two years of schooling that I had missed— Grade Four and Form One. My spoken English wasn't so good, and it took me so many years and hard work to recover.

When I was about to complete Form Three, at the end of 1989, I came across a certain magazine whose name I no longer recall. It was in that old magazine in which I read about an organization called Friends of the Children of Zimbabwe (Shamwari Dzevana VeZimbabwe), which offered scholarships to the less privileged students. I wrote them a letter, and they advised me to apply. Another miracle! I got the scholarship. They agreed to sponsor me for a year. So, in 1990, they paid all my fees including the Ordinary Level examination fee. This award gave me the peace of mind that I had never dreamt of. The knowledge that all my school fees had been paid encouraged me to concentrate on my studies.

Of course, I had other challenges. At that juncture, my pair of shoes had become irreparable. Like some of the students in the school, I walked to school barefooted. That wasn't the hardest part. The worst challenge of having no shoes was encountered when using the school Blair toilet (pit latrine). One had to step on the messed-up floor as if it were a carpet. We all survived that filth.

I Became the School Head Boy

Then, something that I will never forget happened at the beginning of 1990. I received a voucher from Friends of the Children of Zimbabwe, the organization that had offered me a scholarship. That was the first, coupon that I had ever seen in my life. The headmaster explained to me what it was. I was supposed to go to any Bata Shoe outlet and exchange that piece of paper for a pair of shoes. I couldn't believe my ears. It took me some days to convince my mother to give me some bus fare to go to Masvingo, which was the nearest town where I could exchange the voucher for shoes.

This incident will always be inscribed in my mind because I had no shoes at that point, and rumor had it that I stood a better chance of being elected the school head boy. Although there was some truth to that story, I couldn't imagine any sane teacher voting a barefooted boy to be the head of the school prefects. The preferred student was Sydney Mavodza, who had already distinguished himself in the school as the leader of the Church of Christ Choir, which occasionally sang inspiring hymns during school assemblies. He had other relevant attributes too. He was smart, handsome, and intelligent. Vushe Mangezi and Denford Mapuru were other candidates who possessed the desired leadership and academic qualities, but, they didn't make it.

Then, the unexpected happened—I was elected the 1990 school head boy at Mudarikwa Secondary School. Being selected the school head boy wasn't a mean achievement. It was serendipitous that I received the voucher when we were waiting for the installation. It was my year, for I got the scholarship, a pair of shoes, and the position of head boy. The pair of shoes took me through 1990 and beyond. As a staunch Catholic, I believed that those blessings were miracles from God.

Two memorable incidents happened when I was the head boy. First, the school bought our first national flag. I was the first to hoist that flag, after having been trained by Mr. Mutamba, who at that point, had become the deputy headmaster. During that time of unwavering patriotism, getting an opportunity to raise the national flag wasn't a mean achievement. It also became my responsibility to train other school prefects to raise the flag at the beginning of every school day and taking it down at the end of the day. Those were golden moments.

The other incident wasn't a pleasant one. There was a soccer match between our school and Madzivanyika Secondary School. The game was scheduled for a Saturday afternoon. The soccer coach who was perhaps the sports master as well ordered all the students to be at the school early in the morning although the tournament wouldn't start until the afternoon. He was disappointed because only a few students arrived on the stipulated time. It wasn't reasonable for the students to turn up early in the morning for a soccer match that would be in the afternoon. Most students defied the overzealous soccer coach.

Monday came, and the coach decided to punish all students who had arrived for the Saturday match late, although in time for the game. We were all gathered at the assembly point, where we received a sermon from the coach. He started beating up students, class by class. I was exempted from the beating since I was the head boy. Then the unexpected happened. The Form Four class to which I belonged refused to take the corporal punishment. As far as I can remember that action was unprecedented at Mudarikwa Secondary School. The students just walked away from the assembly point and went into their classroom. For two days, the humiliated coach tried to persuade the students to accept the beating, but they refused.

As the school head boy, I then decided to write a letter to the headmaster complaining about the abuse of the students by the soccer coach. I gave the letter to the head girl to read, edit, and sign, which she did. I then delivered it to Mr. Nyambirai, who had succeeded Mr. Mutamba as the headmaster. In that letter, I told the headmaster that the coach's punishment was unwarranted, cruel, and a violation of the student's rights. I pointed out that the soccer coach was an unqualified teacher, and needed to be restrained by qualified teachers who knew the ministry's regulations about student discipline. This point was heavily contested by the headmaster because he felt that there wasn't a need to mention the caliber of the teacher. He invited the two of us to his office and thanked us for letting him know about the situation on the ground, but severely reprimanded us for mentioning the caliber of the teacher. The abuse stopped.

The coach stopped trying to beat up the Form Four students and was very angry with the writer of the letter. What surprised me was that he didn't believe that I had written the letter even after I told him that I had. He firmly felt that somebody else had written it. I tried to convince him that I had written the letter, but he never believed me until I left the school. He argued that since I was exempted from the beatings, I had no cause to write the letter. I still don't understand why he felt that I couldn't write such a letter because as the school head boy, I represented the students.

He had his own suspects. One of his suspects was one of the students who was tipped to become the head boy but missed it. I told him that there was no way that student could have assisted me to compose that letter because we had ceased to be close friends, or perhaps we never were. Our relationship had been strained by an incident that had happened at the beginning of my tenure as the leader of the school prefects. The student in question was the class monitor and was responsible for putting up a duty roster for the cleaning of the classroom. Since I was the head boy, I assumed that the class monitor would exempt me from doing classroom duties. He didn't. I challenged him and went on to erase my name from his duty roster. I don't think it went down well with him.

Yes, it's I who wrote the letter. I wrote it because I knew that the teacher was wrong. I challenged the coach and the system, and my classmates were saved from the wanton beatings of an unreasonable teacher. I felt that the beatings were unwarranted. Of course, I saved all my classmates except one, who offered himself for the corporal punishment by the coach. This is what happened. For a few days after the Form Four class had refused to take the corporal punishment from the coach, he would come to our classroom every morning, offering his shameful abuse. The students always refused, except one student who offered himself for the torture. He got more than he bargained for, but other students still refused to be beaten.

Mudarikwa Secondary School was an outstanding school, but there were setbacks as well. The school was far away from my home. I had to run along the way to arrive early for classes. In addition to that, most of the teachers weren't trained to teach at secondary schools. Be that as it may, they were excellent and well-meaning teachers. When we got to Form Four, we didn't have a History teacher although we had registered to write the History examination. We had to study for the exam alone. The headmaster was the Science teacher, but seldom attended classes. The most faithful and dedicated teachers were the Mathematics, Shona language, and Commerce teacher. We set for our Ordinary Level examinations, and I passed with flying colors. I think that our record at Mudarikwa still stands unbroken to date. I finished my secondary school education, at least one year behind my original schedule.

Completing secondary education wasn't easy for me. There were so many challenges that I encountered on the way. There were times when I despaired and almost lost hope of ever achieving my goals. I worked hard all the way. I also got good counsel from employers and friends. Those people who ill-treated me, in fact, strengthened my focus and determination. I believed that I was treated like that because I wasn't educated. I convinced myself that I had to educate myself to reclaim my humanity and dignity.

Now that I hold a doctoral degree, do I feel satisfied? That is a story for another day. I sometimes tell my children that I never had a table on which to study until I finished Form Four. Most of the times, I went to school without shoes. That most of the times I went to school without having eaten anything. That I had no warm jersey until I finished High School. My children look at me in utter puzzlement. They don't understand how one can go to school without shoes. It inconceivable for them to comprehend why one had to walk such a long distance to school. They don't understand how a student can finish High School without a desk on which to write homework. Of course, my struggle for education wasn't unique. Some students were worse off than I. At least, some of my dreams were realized, but most of my friends' efforts never paid off. I haven't achieved much, but considering where I started, and where I am right now, I can't complain much. God and his people have been good to me.

CHAPTER 4

MY SPIRITUAL AWAKENING

The Old Bible

My spiritual awakening happened at the end of Zimbabwe's Liberation War, in 1979. During the War, the rural people had been forbidden from attending church services by the freedom fighters, who claimed that Christianity was the religion of White people, whose God was also White. Before the War, there was only one predominant Christian denomination in Nyajena; the Dutch Reformed Church. Its followers had built a massive church near Nyajena Primary School, perhaps one of the only two church buildings in Nyajena. The other church building, whose existence I didn't know about until long after the War, was the Roman Catholic Church at Zorogwe, in the area of Chief Nyamande. I had passed by the impressive Dutch Reformed church at Nyajena on several occasions, but I had never set my foot in it.

Although the Dutch Reformed Church had built only one church in Nyajena, its adherents weren't deprived of the places in which they could hold church services. All other congregations gathered for worship in classrooms at almost every primary school in Nyajena. The believers from my village worshipped at Chitakai Primary School. I am told that there was a time when all school pupils had to attend the Sunday services at Chitakai School, and there would be a student leader, or teacher who would record their attendance. Those students who missed Sunday services would be punished by the teachers. Consequently, almost every villager could sing the Dutch Reformed Church hymns.

Of course, some other church denominations were making inroads into Nyajena when the War started. For instance, the Zion Christian Church, and the other Zionist Churches were becoming popular. I knew of Mr. Edias Mavodza and Mr. Maramwidze (VaChitavate) who were adherents of the Zion Christian Church. As kids, we used to go to Mr. Edias Mavodza's home to watch the Zionist dance. It was a lively dance, and I loved it.

Then, the War came, and Christians were prevented from attending church services. The freedom fighters (comrades) told people that God was white, and as such, was the enemy of the people. Attending church services became a pernicious political crime. So, the believers stopped going to church. Moreover, Chitakai School, where they used to congregate was utterly destroyed. Other schools were damaged too except a couple of them, such as Chiwawa Primary school, which survived because of its proximity to Renco Mine. The church at Nyajena had its roof ripped off except for the pinnacle.

The freedom fighters knew that they couldn't just take away the people's religion without replacing it with something. They encouraged people to turn to their ancestors for blessings, oracles, and protection. Of course, ancestor veneration had existed before the War, but the freedom fighters gave it an impetus that we had never experienced before. First, they claimed that they were the children of Ambuya Nehanda, a spirit medium whose host was Nyakasikana, who was hanged by the British in 1897 for having led the First Chimurenga. She is the woman who is reported to have refused to be converted to Christianity by Father Richartz, S.J, just before her execution. She didn't see the rationale of him trying to offer her an everlasting life with one hand while taking her earthly life with the other.

Her counterpart, Sekuru Kaguvi accepted baptism and earned himself the most ungodly name, Dismas. Dismas is believed to have been the name of the famous repentant thief whom Jesus promised Paradise at the eleventh hour, on the Cross. I have always wondered why in Christ's holy name, any priest would think that Dismas was the right name for somebody who had been arrested while defending his country and people from the oppression and exploitation of the white settlers. There were so many biblical characters whose names could have been appropriate for a convert such as Kaguvi, but the priest chose the name, Dismas. How about the name Paul, a convert to Christianity, who had been at the forefront in killing Christians for no reason other than that they were different? How about the name David, the second Israelite King who is renowned for having slain the giant Goliath, who had despised the people of God? The same giant's slayer had also caused the death of one of his soldiers, Uriah, to snatch away his wife, Bathsheba. Be that as it may, Sekuru Kaguvi died Dismas, perhaps the last time ever that name was used for any Christian convert in Zimbabwe.

The comrades composed songs in which Nehanda and other Liberation War heroes were somewhat deified. Some of the tunes were plagiarized from the old church hymns. In some songs, it was said that Nehanda had instructed the Zimbabwean people to take up arms to defeat the white people. The songs were sung during *pungwe* meetings (night vigils) to boost the fighters' morale.

Overnight, many people turned to ancestor veneration. In our village, there were spirit mediums such as *Sekuru* Mugumo, who gave the freedom fighters directions in military and spiritual matters. Many adults got themselves snuff containers that were made of cow horns in which they stored ground tobacco. This ground tobacco was used to appease the ancestors. The beer was brewed for the ancestors, and a libation poured for them. Children sang ancestral hymns as they herded goats. Nobody talked about the Christian God. It seemed like God was dead.

So, what happened that ignited the fear of the forbidden Christian God in me? We found an old bible that belonged to my mother's sister who had taken her own life. We really don't know why she decided to take matters into her own hands, but she did. No one has ever explained it to me, but as I continue to reflect upon the fateful events that took place just before she killed herself, I have a reconstruction of what might have caused her untimely demise. At the Svimborume base attack, my aunt's daughter, Perekai, had died. After the onslaught, most people ran away from the village, but those villagers whose relatives had died had to stay at home to make burial arrangements for their beloved ones. The following morning after the attack, the Rhodesian army that was stationed at Muchibwa hospital sent helicopters to our village so that all who had died would be flown to Renco Mine for identification. The corpses were accompanied by their next of kin. My aunt with her last born Sostina was flown to Renco Mine to identify Perekai's body. After that, they were returned back home by the same helicopter. My aunt's tribulations started just after that horrendous and unprecedented trip aboard the enemy's helicopter.

"How does one board the enemy's helicopter without "selling out" the secrets of the freedom fighters?" The freedom fighters wanted to know. That question haunted my aunt for several days before her death. The freedom fighters put her on the death row. They kept promising her that they would kill her during their next visit, and she waited. We also waited in utter fear. There was nothing she could do but wait. It's only now that I realize that she had another option—running away. Most victims never saw that opportunity because they had been brainwashed. They were told that wherever they went, they would be apprehended and executed. Like other victims, my aunt waited. I can't imagine how she might have felt, just waiting for her execution.

When the freedom fighters kept postponing her death, she could no longer bear the waiting anymore. She took her own life. If my reconstruction is accurate, I think that my mother, uncles, and cousins were relieved that she had braved the winds and taken things into her own hands. She had escaped the gruesome, slow, and disgraceful death that she would have faced from the freedom fighters. She had saved her family from the sad and heart-rending experiences of witnessing the execution of their beloved relative without being able to openly mourn her. She had beaten the freedom fighters at their own game. Some readers might think that I support suicide; I don't. I am writing about a war situation in which it became heroic for a besieged warrior to deprive her enemy of having the pleasure of tormenting her. I am writing about a scenario in which the victim's body could be dismembered part by part until he or she died. My aunt escaped that torture, but death is death, it doesn't matter how it comes.

Looking at my aunt's death from another angle, I think that if she had received counseling, she could have found other alternatives. Some people in situations like hers escaped and joined their relatives in cities, far from the treacherous crowd. That way, they survived the brutalities of the revolution that in some cases, enjoyed devouring its own children. In most cases, if not all, killing oneself doesn't solve problems. In fact, it creates more problems for others. My aunt's children were left with no one to care for them. Our lives don't only belong to us, but also to our families, community, and God. Life shouldn't be taken by anyone for any reason except God. When faced with grievous dangers, it's always wiser to fight until we breathe our last.

I Became a Roman Catholic

Anyway, we got her old bible and my mother and brother Emmanuel, read it to us. I really enjoyed listening to the stories because I was hearing them for the first time. The old bible was the only book that was in the house, and my brother did an excellent job of narrating some of the stories that he would have read during the day in our absence. Every evening became a story-telling ritual, and Emmanuel became our sacred practitioner. The stories touched me so much that I felt I needed such a mighty God in my life. The horrors and vulnerabilities caused by the War had taught me that only an invincible being such as God was capable of giving me the protection that I needed. I had lost my trust in the protection of the freedom fighters.

I started praying alone silently. Nobody taught me how to pray, but I composed my own prayers. I might have read a couple of prayers, but I can't recall where I had read them. I prayed at night silently every day before I went to sleep. The pictures of God that I had in my mind were of my own making. They were shaped by the biblical stories that Emmanuel narrated every evening.

Then 1980 brought us our independence from the colonial rule, and everything went back to normal. People went back to the type of life that they had led before the War. Schools were reopened, and Christianity resurrected from its long slumber. One of the first churches to be revived was the Dutch Reformed Church, which resumed its worship services at Chitakai Primary School. Although some of my classmates became members of that denomination, I never felt the need to attend its services. Then, my friend Emmanuel Marapira told me about a new church that had just started at Chitakai School—the Roman Catholic Church. The leader of that church was Mr. Petros Mahweta, a young man who was full of vision, zeal, and passion.

Many of my other friends also encouraged me to attend the new church. I did, and I liked it.

That might have been at the beginning of 1983.

On my very first attendance, Fr. Graf, a priest who was stationed at Bondolfi Mission came to celebrate Mass for us. That was my first time to see a white man at close range. I mean a different and caring one. A white man who could speak the people's language, eat *mubovora* (pumpkin leaves), and drink *mukumbi* (Amarula juice). That was the last day I ever saw him because he was soon replaced by Fr. Josef Haag, who was stationed at Triangle at that time. Later, Fr. Haag came to stay at Saint Barbara, Renco Mine. From that day, I have never looked back. Before the Liberation War, the Roman Catholic Church was only in Magudu area. They had built a Primary School, Zorogwe, and a church in that area. But both were destroyed during the War.

I started volunteering to do Sunday readings at our parish. I was a good reader. I also began learning catechism the same year and was baptized at Chitakai School by fr. Haag in 1984. I was confirmed a week later by the late bishop of Gweru Diocese, Tobias Wunganai Chiginya, at Saint Barbara, Renco Mine. My friend, Emmanuel Marapira, soon left the Catholic Church to join the Jack of All Nations Church popularly known as Jangamishoni. That Church had been brought to Mavuka's village by a certain Mapipi, who worked as a domestic worker at one of the villagers.

The Jangamishoni Church stole several Catholic youths from our parish. One of such youths was Kenneth Muganji, together with all his sisters and cousins. Many other friends from my church also left the Roman Catholic Church for other churches. But, I kept the Catholic faith. In fact, at some point, I became overzealous about the Catholic faith. I started volunteering to teach catechism when I was in Form Two, in 1988. I also became interested in preaching, and it seemed that I had a talent in that area. I sang and beat the drums although I wasn't a good singer. At Saint Teresa, there were better singers such as Walter Chidembo and Mr. Mahweta.

In 1987, the Catholic Church moved from Chitakai School to Guwa Township where we were building our new church. I think that the church was completed in 1988, and was consecrated by the late Bishop Francis Mugadzi. Fr. Josef Haag provided most of the funds that were used to build the church, but the parishioners provided the labor. The youth formed the bricks that were used to make the church. Building a church wasn't a simple thing, but we had the faith. With faith nothing is impossible. We were young and had the energy and the passion. And we built our own church.

Mr. Matapura, a devout Catholic, and a businessman, who was stationed at Guwa used his lorry to fetch the water needed for the construction. We worked so hard that each time I look at the church, I am perplexed by what the determination of a united people can achieve. I marvel at fellow youths who toiled at that church such as

Vitalis Mutinha, Hosea Mutinha, Thomas Tsvuke, Leonard Tsvuke, Tapiwa Madakuchekwa, Miriam Munikwa, Chipo Zivave, Shamiso Mavuku, Clever Chiramba, Joshua Mutinha, Svunurai Chafuka, and many others whose names I can't recall. Building Saint Teresa wasn't an easy task, but our unshakable faith, the oneness of purpose, and unwavering dedication made it possible.

I Entered the Seminary

From an early stage in my Catholic faith development, I had always wanted to become a priest. I was aware of the challenges and sacrifices to be made, but that's what I wanted to be. So, as I struggled to get an education, I aimed at getting into the priesthood. Because of the celibacy requirement, my colleagues and teachers laughed at my ambition, but I was determined.

In 1991, as soon as I got my Ordinary Level results, I was ready to go to seminary. I started the application process. I don't know how I had come to know about the Franciscan Friars who were stationed at Saint Francis of Assisi Mission in Chivhu. I think that the Holy Cross Sisters at Renco Mine might have told me about them. I applied and was invited to what they called a Live-in workshop, where they told us about their way of life. This didn't go down well with Fr. Haag who wanted me to join the Diocesan priesthood. There was nothing that he could do to stop me because I was free to do what I wanted with my life.

At the Franciscan Live-in, I met Father Phillip Timmons O.F.M. who became my main attraction in the Franciscan Order at that time. He appeared to be so holy, no wonder he became a prominent attraction to most of the aspirants. I remember only two of the many aspirants that gathered at Nharira Mission that August of 1990. There was the late Patrick Gumbo, who later joined the diocesan seminary, and died in a car accident in which Fr. Urayai's car was swept away by an overflowing river. Fr. Urayai survived. May the good lord bless Patrick's soul, for he was an excellent young man. There was also Martin Mazango, who later joined the Friars and left during his early years of formation.

At the beginning of 1991, I was invited to an interview at Assisi. Again, I met Patrick Gumbo at that interview. After two days, Brother Peter (not his real name), who was the postulant master explained to me that Patrick was found wanting in some areas that he didn't divulge to me. Consequently, he was rejected by the interviewers, who included one religious nun. The rejection of Patrick was a big blow to me for two reasons. First, he and I had become friends in those two days we had spent together at Assisi. Second, I had to wait for another year to join the Friars because I couldn't start the Franciscan formation alone. I had to wait until they got the required number of postulants. The primary challenge was that there was no guarantee that even if I waited for a year, the Friars would find enough candidates to open the postulancy the following year. I felt that the wait would be too long unless I were assured that the postulancy would begin in 1992. Brother Peter wasn't willing to make any promises, and I was disappointed. I was young, unwise, impatient, and impetuous. For me, a whole year was tantamount to all eternity.

I went back home to Nyajena, full of disappointment. I immediately contacted Fr. Haag, who was thrilled to know that I had decided to join the diocesan priesthood. Within a week, all the necessary arrangements were made, and I went to Chikwingwizha Minor Seminary where all the other candidates had gathered. I arrived at Chikwingwizha Minor Seminary late at night, and Fr. Nyatsanza, who was the rector, wasn't amused. At Chikwingwizha, I met people such as Simon Chaputsira, who we later nicknamed, Musande because of his deep spirituality. I also met the late Fr. Peter Rugora, who later became the rector of Chiwashasha Seminary. There were Alois Madumbu and Charles Mashamba, the inseparable friends, who had met each other in their earlier calling, at Assisi. There was also John Fisher, whose eyeglasses' lenses were so thick that I felt pity for him. I don't want to forget Terence Nyandoro, who we later nicknamed, Speedometer because of his enthusiastic and inspiring way of doing things. There were also Patrick Makwara and Francis Chaurura, who had been educated at Chikwingwizha Minor Seminary, in Gweru. The two were good friends.

The following day, we left Chikwingwizha for Harare by train. The next morning, we arrived at Campion House (cathedral), in Harare, where we met other seminarians from all over Zimbabwe, including one from Botswana. That same day, we walked to Rockwood Spiritual Center that is situated in Hatfield, Harare. That was my first time in Harare, and I was just following others without any awareness of where I was. At Rockwood, we met Fr. Raymond Kapito, SJ (is late now), who would become our formator and the rector at the new Spiritual Formation Center at Mazowe. His team also included Father Hummel, SMB, and Fr. Peter Mufaro, a diocesan priest from Gweru Diocese.

At Rockwood, we were packed like sardines in the few bedrooms that we shared. Soon, Fr. Kapito elected the leaders of the group, the most powerful being the beadle and his deputy. We stayed at Rockwood for just a couple of weeks before we moved to Mbebi, in Mazowe, which would become our permanent home for that year. Just before we left Rockwood, Brother Peter, who had become aware that I had joined the Diocesan seminary came to visit me. I told him that I couldn't wait indefinitely for the Franciscans to find the sufficient number of candidates. He gave me a gift of $20.00, which at that time was a lot of money. I appreciated his generosity because I didn't have any pocket money.

There are two things that I will never forget that happened when we were at Rockwood. First, one of the Harare seminarians who was the deputy to the beadle tried to wrestle the leadership of the group from the beadle, who was a seminarian from Bulawayo Diocese. It didn't end there. The vice beadle, being a product of the only archdiocesan at the time, claimed to know everything. He started harassing and oppressing other students.

I will never forget the day he poured onto the ground a big pot of tea because we hadn't done the general work to his satisfaction. Yes, I said a big bowl of tea. His mean and uncalled-for gesture was appalling to me because where I came from tea was sacred, and wasn't supposed to be wasted in that manner. We only drank tea at Christmas. I couldn't understand why a seminarian would deprive others of that rare liquid. In fact, that guy became a dictator within a few days. Be that as it may, his cruelty was to be short-lived because someone reported him to Fr. Kapito, who immediately convened a meeting. It wasn't I who informed about him. At that meeting, which all the seminarians attended, he was humiliated and reduced to his deputizing position. I had never seen such frankness before. Of course, I never said a word in that meeting, and that is why it took me many months to forgive him. We were all relieved after the meeting.

The second issue involved a seminarian who came from my home area, Nyajena. One day, someone saw him crying while sitting on top of the rock that some people claimed to be sacred. Since he was my homeboy, some people told me about his depression, and I went up there to talk with him. He was so upset and was thinking of leaving the seminary. He said that he had no clothes, money, and other basic necessities. I felt sad for him. I gave him two of the three shirts that Fr. Haag had given me. I had to because he was worse off than I was, and I wanted him to stay in the seminary. He stayed and made it to the priesthood. Unfortunately, he was expelled by the bishop several years after his ordination for reasons that I don't know. As I reflect on the incident now, I understand why he was so sad about his lack of appropriate clothing. He had just come from high school, and his best clothes were his school uniform, yet other seminarians changed clothes every day.

Eventually, we went to Mazowe where many big surprises were awaiting me. We cooked our own food, and there was always a scramble for meat. We were overcrowded in the dormitories. Mass was celebrated every day and was followed by the lessons. Fr. Raymond Kapito, SJ was the rector. He was a very educated priest and a man of deep spirituality. The life at the Spiritual Formation Center was like at a boarding school. I was so quiet, and Fr. Kapito always picked on me. I didn't entirely trust my mastery of the English language, so I was scared to talk in class. Other seminarians were very fluent in the Queen's language because they had been educated at better schools. When the teasing from Fr. Kapito became unbearable for me, I surprised him. One day, I went to his office and complained about his teasing.

"Fr. I think that you hate me. Every time you pick on me. You try to prove that I am not as smart as other seminarians, yet I know that I am smarter than most of the seminarians." I caught him unawares. He was mesmerized and was quiet for a moment.

"I am sorry if my comments make you feel that way. In fact, I love you so much, just like I love every other seminarian here. I know that you are smarter than most of the seminarians here. That's why I encourage you to become the best you can."

He then gave me a book that was titled, *The Unconditional Love* written by John Powell. Until now, I don't know how I gathered the energy to speak with Fr. Kapito like I did, but it helped. He stopped teasing me but was spying on me, through some seminarians. Eventually, I started participating actively in class discussions and the liturgy. I even began leading in singing. I remember very well the first day I sang. It was after our night prayers, and I sang the closing hymn. Fr. Kapito, who was about to exit the room stopped, looked at me, and smiled. I could tell that he was glad that I had finally moved out of my cocoon. I survived that year.

Leaving the Seminary

The following year (1992) I failed to raise enough money to go to the seminary to study philosophy. If you have never been in the same economic place as I was, you wouldn't understand why I had to drop out of the seminary because of poverty. In Zimbabwe, seminary education was paid for by the bishops, so I may say it was for free from the seminarian's point of view. But, there were many other things that some bishops didn't provide for the seminarians that belonged to their dioceses. For instance, some bishops didn't buy books, clothes, shoes, soap, and so on for their seminarians.

During my time in high school, I had gone without most of these necessities, but the seminary was different. Things like shoes, appropriate clothes, bus fare, and others had become necessities. On top of that, other seminarians had them. I wrote a letter to one of the priests, who at that time was the Vicar General of Gweru diocese. I explained my dire situation to him, which I think he understood. He responded and said that he would verify my financial condition from my Parish Priest, Fr. Josef Haag. He never came back to me. Father Haag also never came back to me. I didn't make a follow up with Fr. Haag because I felt that he knew my situation. He had been my parish priest for several years. He had visited my home. When I first went to the seminary, he had given me three shirts and a pair of pajamas. Moreover, Fr. Haag had friends in Germany who could assist me if he requested it, yet he didn't. I just concluded that he didn't care about my condition, and I wouldn't bother him.

During one of the seminary vacations, I went to Zvishavane and looked for a temporary job so that I could raise some money for my bus fare and upkeep at the seminary. I wasn't lucky. I lived with my uncle, his son, and two nephews of his, who also worked in the mine. Life was so difficult. My uncle would buy a 50-kg bag of mealie meal at the end of every month, and no vegetables. He expected his son and nephews to buy meat or vegetables, which they didn't. For the first time, I ate *sadza* without veggies.

For two months, I would go to Saint Joseph's Catholic Church to pray. I prayed for a miracle. I wanted God to give me a job so that I would be able to go back to the seminary. No miracle happened. Miracles don't occur when you want them to happen. They wait for their own time. I met the parish priest of Saint Joseph's Catholic Church at the church a couple of times. On one occasion he asked me if everything was okay, and I said it was. I still don't know why I didn't share my financial challenges with him. I always felt that I shouldn't bother people with my problems. I also didn't have the skills of negotiating with people. I thought that people were supposed to know what I needed. It was their responsibility to discover what I lacked. I was wrong. They weren't prophets.

This way of thinking had been detrimental to my success as a soccer player at the seminary. I couldn't ask for or demand the ball as other players did. I wasn't used to demanding things that I thought were supposed to be given to me without me asking. I would take what was offered to me. I felt that it was my teammates' responsibility to see my vantage point and pass the ball to me. They never did, and I was so frustrated. I challenged one of the seminarians, Alluwis Hatirarami.

"I am not going to play soccer anymore," I said to him.

"Why not? You are such a good player?" He wanted to know.

"Nobody ever passes the ball to me. You people are so selfish. When you get the ball, you only look for your friends," I complained. I still think that to some extent my allegations were justified. Those readers who play social soccer might know that there are times when a few players only pass the ball to their friends.

"The problem with you John is that you think that you are so special. You don't ask for the ball. We pass the ball to people who demand it. If you want to be a good soccer player, you have to humble yourself and ask for the ball. That's what all of us do." He was right. Alluwis had given me an accurate analysis of who I was. It's not that I didn't ask for the ball, I did—one or two times, and if it weren't passed to me, I would stop asking. It wasn't only about asking for the ball, it was about asking in general. I didn't know how to persist in asking for something. If I asked for something once, and it wasn't granted, I would take that as a no. I didn't know how to verify my assumptions with the people concerned. If I felt that someone didn't like me, then that was it. If I thought that someone was taking advantage of me, I didn't know how to check that with him or her. I didn't know how to fight for my rights. My popular option was just to say nothing or walk away. With hindsight, I think that I suffered from inferiority complex and lack of confidence, which manifested itself as humility.

I Joined Saint Paul's Brother

I decided to leave the diocese and join the Saint Paul's Brothers. I had met one of the Saint Paul's Brothers at one of the vocation workshops at Gokomere High School a couple of years before I went to seminary. Moreover, one of my colleagues at the seminary had told me that if one joined the brothers, they would take care of his personal needs. At the beginning of 1992, I got on a bus from Zvishavane to Gweru. When I got to Gweru, I called the Saint Paul's Brothers, and within thirty minutes, one of the brothers arrived to pick me up. The response was so fast that I was impressed. It was like they were expecting me. I later discovered that the brothers thought I was one of their candidates for whom they had been waiting on that day. I explained my issue to them, and they listened. They accepted me into the candidacy, and I was grateful. For a couple of weeks, I was so confused and disoriented that I couldn't remember directions to different rooms in the big house. The thought of leaving the seminary had left me mentally exhausted and confused. My thoughts were foggy. I was utterly fragile when I got to Saint Paul's House, in Gweru. If I hadn't gone to Gweru at the time that I did, I could have gone out of my mind.

Leaving the seminary was a devastating decision because I really wanted to become a priest. I had dreamt of becoming a priest throughout my high school. I also thought of people who knew about me and had supported me in pursuing my vocation. I thought of my friends. I didn't know how to get out of the seminary without becoming a laughing stock of the society. In Zimbabwe, people are taught about how to get into religious life, and not about how to get out of it. I didn't want to disappoint people. Yet, I couldn't continue with the seminary because I couldn't afford the few expenses that I was supposed to meet. It may not make any sense to someone that a person may drop out of the seminary because of the lack of bus fare to get back to seminary, but that's what happened.

The love and acceptance that I received from the Saint Paul's Brothers contributed to my swift recovery. Within about three weeks the fog that had clouded my thinking was cleared. I felt that I had made the right decision. I learned a lot of things at Saint Paul's House. I learned how to garden, cook, clean the house, and raise chickens. *Sekuru* Zhizha was the general handyman. He was such a beautiful soul who had a peaceful, non-anxious, and calm presence. He was patient and hardworking too. I never witnessed him losing his temper during my entire stay at Saint Paul's House. He taught me to love gardening. He showed me how to prevent tomato plants from getting diseases.

Sekuru Grey, the cook, was different. Although he was a nice gentleman and an excellent cook, he lacked the gentleness of *mudhara* Zhizha. Mr. Grey could treat you rough if he felt you were tampering with his kitchen. Yes, he was an excellent cook. Unlike at Mazowe, where we scrambled for food, the brothers had more than enough food. In fact, their diet was more of prodigality than necessity. We worked, ate, prayed, and played sports, particularly, soccer and volleyball. We even competed with neighboring teams and defeated them. I was good at the first three activities, and not quite good at soccer playing.

Soon, I discovered that something was amiss at Saint Paul's House. The brothers didn't take care of the candidates' personal needs. Of cause, we got soap, gumboots, overalls, and skin lotions, but nothing more. There were no stipends for candidates. At one time, I desperately needed a pair of shoes because my old pair had worn out. Both soles were riddled with nails to the extent that whenever I was walking, I would stop from time to time fixing the pins that were pricking my feet from inside the shoes. I will never forget when one of the brothers jokingly told me that my old shoes were destroying the floor of the chapel because of the nails. He was right. I wasn't angry, but embarrassed. As I retrospectively look at that incident now, I know he was right. He was the finally-professed brother who required me once or twice every week to get into his bedroom and polish his shoes. The assignment usually took me an hour or so because he had so many pairs of quality shoes that he hardly had enough space for in his room, yet I didn't have even a single reliable pair of shoes.

As my shoes became worse and almost beyond repair, I never thought of asking for money to buy shoes from the brothers, or the priest who was in-charge. I thought that the brothers knew what I needed, and it was their responsibility to observe that I needed shoes. They saw it but didn't care much about it. I then decided to do the unthinkable. I wrote a letter to the parishioners of my home church, Saint Teresa's Guwa, asking for some money to buy shoes. I don't think that I expected them to do anything about it because the parish was so poor. Why did I request for money from them? I believe that it was a result of the confusion of my being in need. As I had feared, nobody responded. Yes, they got the letter, but nobody cared to acknowledge. I didn't hold that against them. I knew that they had no obligation to assist me because they weren't responsible for my upkeep. The brothers were. We worked so hard at Saint Paul's that we deserved a small stipend. I think that if I had asked the brothers for a pair of shoes, they would have provided me with the money. I didn't. It was my fault.

Instead, I asked the poor parishioners of Saint Teresa's Church. I later regretted having asked them to assist me. This is what happened. About two years after I had left the Saint Paul's Brothers, I boarded the same bus with one of my high school headmasters. At that time, he was heading Makumbe Primary School. I can't remember how we happened to sit in the same seat. "John, I was told that you wrote a letter to the members of Saint Theresa's Church asking for some money to buy shoes?" That's how it started. "John, you have no shame. You are a brilliant young man. You passed your Ordinary Level with flying colors. Then, you refused to go to college or look for a job. You decided to become a priest. You left the seminary and joined the brothers. Now you ask the poor people of Saint Theresa to assist you? You are a big disgrace to the school. I am distraught with you. You know how poor your mother and siblings are. How she struggled to send you to school. You finish school, and then you decide not to work. In your right mind, where do you think the people of Saint Theresa can get money from?" I didn't answer. I think he didn't expect me to respond. I felt sorry for my stupidity. He was right. He was so right. I just looked at him and apologized, but he wasn't yet appeased.

"So, for how long you will continue to beg from people because you don't want to work? You are an embarrassment to all the people who helped you to complete your high school. We all thought that you would be able to stand on your two feet and support your family. But what you do is going to your stupid the seminary. As if that wasn't unwise enough, you ask for assistance from the people who expect you to assist them. That's not what we taught you at Mudarikwa. My advice to you is this; leave that nonsense, and find yourself a job so that you take care of yourself, your mother, and siblings." The conversation ended. I thanked him, but I never stopped thinking about what he said. He was right, and he had every right to give me advice. When I was in high school, he had written reference letters for me on many occasions. He knew me from the time when I worked at Mr. Matapura. He knew every one of my struggles. I knew him very well too. Occasionally, I worked as a barman at Mr. Matapura's beerhall at Guwa Township. That headmaster was one of our regular patrons. He was a good man and inspiring leader.

So, how did I get my next pair of shoes? I did, of course, miraculously. Brother John Buckert, SMB, who was both the novice Director and chief fundraiser for the brothers noticed my need and gave me a pair of his own shoes. They were new and exactly my shoe size. So, the shoe issue was resolved, at least, for now. But, I had other grievances. When I started candidacy at Saint Paul, the brothers had told me that since I had completed a year of spiritual formation at Mazowe, I would just do one year of candidacy, and would skip the one year of Postulancy, entering the Novitiate with the group that was a year ahead of my team. When the year (1992) ended, the brothers changed the goal posts. They told me that there was no hurry for me to get into the novitiate. They said that I had to do the Postulancy just like any other candidate. I was disappointed because they had misled me. I felt betrayed and let down. To worsen the matter, they didn't tell me that I was found wanting in any respect. I thought that they wanted to make use of me because I was a very hard worker who meticulously completed every task that was assigned to me. If I were to join the Novitiate the following year (1993), then I wouldn't be working for the brothers, but the Novitiate, which was on the same premises. I felt that the year of Postulancy would be a waste of time for me since there was no spiritual formation taking place at Saint Paul's for the first two years. The only religious formation one received for the first two years at Saint Paul's was the daily Mass and morning prayers. Most of the time was dedicated to working—cleaning the house, gardening, feeding the chickens, and taking charge of the sacristy. I wanted to move on in my formation. They had promised me. But they had changed their minds. They blocked my getting into Novitiate.

I could have negotiated my case, but I wasn't a good negotiator. In fact, I never tried. The only solution that I thought of was to leave the Saint Paul's Brothers. When I look back at my life, I see that pattern of fleeing without putting up a fight. I thought that it was a sound strategy only to discover that I have lost many opportunities in life by making it easier for other people by quitting without a fight. Of course, there are times when one knows that leaving is the only way out, but I made fleeing my only solution to challenges. There are times when we conquer by fighting. I didn't know how to fight for my rights. I was so upset that they had acted hypocritically. They had no reasons for disallowing me to skip the year of Postulancy. They just said that they had decided against it. Immediately, I started a conversation with the Franciscans, in Chivhu. I had stayed in touch with them all those past two years, and I still felt called to their spirituality. At the end of 1992, I decided to leave the Saint Paul's Brothers, and join the Franciscans in Chivhu. I left in the morning. Father Mutasa dropped me off at the bus terminus in Gweru. He gave me enough money for my bus fare home. In fact, he asked me how much I wanted, and I asked for enough money for my bus fare.

I Joined the Franciscans

When I arrived at Saint Francis of Assisi Postulancy, at the beginning of 1993, I joined four other boys who had been with the Franciscans for a year. There was Theo (not his real name), who later joined the Diocese of Gweru, and at some point, became the Vicar General for the Diocese. He was a brilliant young man who had been educated at Holy Cross Mission. His father was a retired teacher and a very good man. Theo adored him. Theo taught me some basics of the English language that had escaped me in High School. The other postulant was Fidelis Maponde who had hailed from Chitungwiza and was the default leader of the cabal. At times, the Postulant master, Brother Peter, had to intervene on the group's behalf because Fidelis' leadership style had somewhat dictatorial tendencies. I clashed with him on several occasions. However, he was a nice guy and a good footballer. Our clashes were caused by our diametrically opposed backgrounds. He was born and bred in Chitungwiza town, and I was born and bred in Nyajena rural area. It was the clash between the rural and the urban mentalities. We survived each other.

I didn't get to know Martin Mazango and Michael Velapi Chanengeta very well because they were sent home by the Postulant master a couple of months after my arrival. Their dismissal happened one Monday morning. Brother Peter had come back from Harare and told them that they were supposed to leave the postulancy, for they had no vocation to the Franciscan way of life. That's what the duo told us. It was devastating news for both, but Michael quickly recovered from the shock, packed his belongings, and bade us farewell. It seems that he had been accustomed to suffering because when I arrived at Assisi, Michael had been admitted to Muvonde Hospital in Churumanzu because of some persistent stomach problems. He recovered and rejoined us, but he might have known that his days with the Friars were numbered. When he was expelled, he had just recovered and rejoined the group. Michael is the man, who after I had shared my life story with the team, said that I was a great person, and the future had something big in store for me. I have always taken his utterance as a prophecy.

Martin Mazango reacted to the news of his dismissal in an unprecedented manner— he refused to leave. He wanted to know why the Franciscans were saying that he had no Franciscan vocation. Brother Peter made a mistake by telling him that the Holy Spirit had inspired him to know that.

"When the Holy Spirit wanted me to join this congregation, she spoke to me directly. Now that the same Holy Spirit thinks that I have no vocation, it would make a lot of sense to me for she comes to me directly, instead of communicating via you. Is the Holy Spirit now afraid of me because I have no vocation? Brother Peter, when the Holy Spirit tells you that I don't have a vocation, please, redirect her to me. If the Holy Spirit directly tells me that I don't have a vocation, I won't stay here a minute longer." That's how Martin told us he had argued.

We never heard the conversation from Brother Peter's point of view. But, what I know for sure is that Brother Peter was disillusioned. He was so sad, and his skin became so pale. The friars privy to the inside information told us that Brother Peter called his mother in Ireland. From the stories of her that he shared with us, I gathered that he loved her dearly and had been a source of strength and inspiration in his life.

The parish priest also tried to forcibly evict Martin to no avail. We all tried to persuade him to leave, but he wouldn't listen. Sometimes, when he narrated the issue, he would clap his hands and laugh hysterically. After about a week, Martin finally agreed to leave, but after a meeting between the formators and his parents. The Postulants master gave the trio a ride back to their home near Gandachibvuva. We were also asked to accompany them. Martin's father, who was so furious about the dismissal of his son from the Postulancy decided to finish the remaining five or so kilometers of the journey on foot. Thus, the two, Michael and Martin left, and the three of us stayed.

As soon as I arrived at Assisi, I realized that things were different. The food was rationed in a manner that I had never experienced before. Just a small jar of sugar was supposed to last for a week. This is how it worked. Each week, one of us would be in-charge of the kitchen and cooking. That kitchen guy would be responsible for the care of the food items. Since the sugar was too little, he had to give each one of us a spoonful of sugar for our tea. The meat was also in short supply that the cook had to make sure that each one of us picked up a piece at a time while being observed by others. The situation became worse when four other postulants came to join us. Things were more difficult for me, having lived at Saint Paul's where food was plenty. We suffered. I still don't know why the farmators felt that the little food was enough for seven teenage boys. There were no shortages of meat and sugar at that time. Yes, there was a drought in 1992, but the brothers had money, and there was a lot of food on the market. We were young and had excellent appetites, but the food just wasn't enough. Most of the time the bread was stale, but still, we consumed it.

The other issues concerned the dismissal of Martin and Michael. The expulsions brought about the fear of not being in control of one's future. Just to know that the master had the unquestionable and uncontestable authority to send any postulant home for the subjective reason that he didn't have a vocation to religious life, was unbearable for me. For the first time, I really felt vulnerable. I had left both the diocesan seminary and the Saint Paul's Brothers on my own accord, and to think that I could end up like Martin was incomprehensible. We talked about it with other postulants. We even feared to sit in the front of the truck with the master. The safest part of the vehicle was the back, far away from his scrutiny. Only Fidelis, who had an insatiable desire to sit in the front seat dared to do so. Brother Peter read the situation and produced a roster for sitting in the front seat of the car. Every time that I rode in front with Brother Peter, he would find some mistake about me or in how I would have reacted to some of his comments. Through the grace of God, the three of us proceeded to the Novitiate at Gandachibvuva, at the beginning of June 1993.

I think that Brother Peter never knew about our fears. He also wasn't aware that the food wasn't enough, or that the bread was stale. I never gathered enough courage to tell him about it. I thought that as our master, he ought to know that we were afraid, and that the food was insufficient for our untamed appetites. Brother Peter was a good man. He became my lifelong friend. Every time I think of him, I have a feeling that he liked me. He saw something special in me that compelled him to accept me into the Franciscan Order when he knew that I had quit the diocesan seminary and Saint Paul's Brothers. I never gathered enough courage to ask him what he saw in me. Even when I left the Franciscans, he paid for my tuition at Wadzanai Training Center. Later, he assisted me to go to the Catholic Theological Union and took care of my family when I was away. Although we no longer communicate, I will forever have a special place for him in my heart.

Father Philip Timmons was the parish priest of the Gandachibvuva parish when we arrived. Father Sean was the Novice Director. We had our own makeshift apartment that the three of us shared as our bedroom. We had our meals at the parish house together with other friars. Everything went smoothly until the arrival of Father James from Ireland. He came to take up the position of Assistant Novice Director. He was well-meaning except that he had no knowledge of the African culture. We never clashed with him until the Novice Director went to South Africa for a vacation, and left Jim in charge of us. He would secretly watch us as we worked and would record the time each one of us was resting. The primary job was digging up an anthill so that the soil would be used in the vegetable garden. Jim complained that we were lazy and weren't supposed to rest. I don't think he had ever done manual work in his life. I believe that it was very irresponsible for the friars to bring someone who had no understanding of the African culture, and make him Assistant Novice Director without intercultural training.

The incident that brought about a severe clash between Jim and the three of us happened in December of 1993. We were invited by one of the teachers to attend a Christmas party at Govere High School. Theo, who was the leader for the week, sought permission from both Jim and Father Philip, who also had been invited to the same event, separately. The party started about 6:00 pm. After saying the grace, Father Phillip was served his food first and ate it. As soon as he finished eating, he told us that it was time to go back to the mission. We hadn't yet eaten our food. Theo said to him that we would come back to the mission immediately after dinner. Father Phillip agreed and left in his truck. Then, it started raining heavily, and by the time the thunderstorms ended, and it became safe enough to walk back to the mission, it was about 8:00 pm. As soon as we arrived at the mission, we notified Father Jim of our arrival. We went into the chapel to say our evening prayers. As we were coming out of the chapel, we met Father Philip who told us that we weren't supposed to stay at the party until 8:00 pm. We knew that we were in serious trouble.

We anxiously awaited Father Sean's arrival from South Africa. As the Novice Director, he alone could decide our fate. Father Sean arrived back a couple of days after the party incident, and he was so upset when he was told that we had overstayed at the party. He asked each of us to write a report of what had transpired on the day in question. We delayed doing that. We also felt that we had done nothing wrong by staying at the party until 8:00 pm since it was raining.

The first to be summoned to the director's office was Theo, and after about thirty minutes of a closed-door meeting with Father Sean, he came back to our residency bidding us farewell. He had decided to leave the Franciscans. Just like that. I really don't know if Theo was expelled or not, but he told us that he was tired of being interrogated and living in fear and uncertainty. He felt that sooner or later he would be dismissed, so the sooner he left, the better. He had decided to join the diocesan clergy. Fidelis was next to visit the Novice Director's office. He too brought back his academic folder from the novice master's office. He also was going home and was thinking of joining the diocese of Harare. I was the last to be summoned to the director's office. I also asked for my certificates. I was told that if I wanted, I could stay, but I was tired of the uncertainty. I knew that the decision to leave marked the end of my road to religious life. I had tried three different congregations, and things hadn't worked out for me. I felt that it was time to accept defeat.

So, the three of us left, on the same day, and the same bus. I left because they were leaving. I couldn't stand on my own two feet. I couldn't make my personal decision. Later in life, I learned that one shouldn't make decisions based on the whims of a group. Theo went to join Gweru Diocese where he was ordained, and at some point, rose to the Vicariate of the Diocese. Fidelis joined Harare Diocese and eventually left. At some point, he joined the Anglican Church with the intention of becoming an Anglican priest. Again, it wasn't successful. He ended up becoming a high school teacher, which I don't see as a bad thing.

Later, it was said that I had influenced the other boys to leave the novitiate, which wasn't accurate. Frist, I had been to two different religious groups, and the Franciscans were my last bet. I really wanted the boys to stay. Since no one could do the novitiate alone, I could only continue if they remained. Second, both Theo and Fidelis were too smart to be influenced by a person like me. They were different from me. They followed their consciences. Third, I strongly think that they left because of fear. By fear, I am referring to the dismay of uncertainty. The fear of being unable to control their futures. This anxiety had been building up ever since the dismissal of Michael and Martin. The frantic efforts that Martin made to evade expulsion had traumatized us. A couple of weeks before the treacherous party, the director had been talking about the possibility of one of us being dismissed from the Novitiate. We had gone through the first six months of the Novitiate, and he said that he would do the initial assessment as to who would stay or get dismissed. If anyone was to go back home, we all knew who that could be—Theo. Instead of waiting to be sent away, he had to act. I only allowed myself to be influenced. However, I blame no one for my decision to leave the Franciscans. It was my decision. Perhaps God wanted me elsewhere.

I think that God wanted me to be a family man. If I had stayed in religious life, I wouldn't have met the most beautiful woman who has become my best friend and mentor; my wife. I wouldn't have known the pleasure of being a father to two wonderful boys. I thank God for leading me to these people.

CHAPTER 5

FROM WADZANAI TRAINING CENTER TO THE UNIVERSITY OF ZIMBABWE

After leaving the Franciscan novitiate, I didn't know what the future had in store for me. But I was sure of one thing—religious life wasn't meant for me. I had tried three different congregations to no avail. Most of my high school friends were already working or pursuing some kind of professional training. Some of them were already married and had kids. I was far behind professionally, academically, and socially. At that juncture, I felt that I had wasted a lot of time pursuing a mirage. It was like I had responded to a religious call that wasn't intended for me. I regretted the many hours I had spent in chapels doing spiritual exercises when other people were busy studying, working, and making money and kids. I despised myself for being a monumental failure. All that I could see in my future was darkness.

My friends pitied me for two things. First, I had fallen behind regarding professional development. Second, I had become a social outcast. Why a social outcast? In Zimbabwe, when you go to the seminary, people expect you to stay put and become a priest. If you drop out, they think that you have deceived or run away from God. Many people expect God to punish you like the biblical Jonah. Some try to avoid you. Others laugh at you. Of course, there will always be, some who empathize with you.

Was it a waste of time, pursuing religious life? As I look at it now, it wasn't. I now know that all that time I spent meditating, attending daily Masses, and reciting the Divine Office wasn't wasted. It irrevocably transformed me. All the spiritual formation that I went through in those three religious houses molded the person I have become. At Mazowe House of Spiritual Formation, I learned to pray and socialize with others. I also acquired quite a substantial amount of the English

115

vocabulary from the learned, Fr. Raymond Kapito, who had an insatiable penchant for jawbreakers. At Saint Paul's House, I learned to work. Their motto was, *Laborare est orare* (To work is to pray). At Saint Francis of Assisi Postulancy, I learned humility and confidence. At Gandachibvuva Novitiate, I was introduced to a life of humility, contemplation, and service to others. If I hadn't gone through all that spiritual training, I wouldn't be the same person I am now.

Yes, I was confused when I left the Franciscan Novitiate. Brother Peter, again, appearing at a time when I needed him most, had two options for me. He suggested that I could either go to Wadzanai Training Center to train as a catechist or go back to high school to do Advanced Level. I opted for the former. During that time, Wadzanai was under the directorship of the energetic, passionate, visionary, and motherly, Sr. Perpetua Lonergan, PBVM. That year, she was processing applications to make Wadzanai an associate college of Mater Dei Institute of Education in Ireland. If that great arrangement had worked out, Wadzanai graduates would be awarded Diplomas in Education from Mater Dei Institute of Education. That diploma would be recognized as a professional teaching qualification by the government of Zimbabwe.

As students, we didn't quite understand the nitty-gritties of the arrangement, but we felt that it was worth pursuing. After graduating from Wadzanai, we would need a certificate that would bring food to the table. Yes, we were training to be catechists, but in a country whose Catholics only appreciated the work of catechists as volunteers, we needed a more rewarding and recognized qualification. Mater Dei Institute gave us that hope. As part of the requirements, Sister Perpetua recruited a professor from Ireland to teach at Wadzanai Training Center. I don't know what happened to that wonderful plan, but it never worked out. It is likely that, by the time I arrived at Wadzanai Training Center, in 1994, the Mater Dei-Wadzanai conversation had already been dropped, and only existed on the Wadzanai recruitment flyers.

Before the idea entirely collapsed, Sr. Perpetua had already started a conversation with the Department of Religious Studies, Classics, and Philosophy of the University of Zimbabwe, which if successful would see Wadzanai Training Center becoming one of its associate colleges. Graduates of Wadzanai Training Center would be awarded a two-year University of Zimbabwe Diploma in Religious Studies, which would give them two career options. One option would allow graduates to enroll at the University of Zimbabwe, in pursuit of a Bachelor of Arts Honors degree in Religious Studies. Those students, whose ancestors were active enough, would even qualify for a one-year exemption from a three-year program. I qualified for that one-year exemption. The other option enabled graduates to join the Ministry of Education as temporary or semi-qualified teachers under an indefinite teaching contract. Those who opted for this option would register with the Ministry of Education, Sports, and

Culture, about six months before graduation so that they would be deployed to secondary schools that needed their services. I opted for the former.

Wadzanai was granted the associate status by the University of Zimbabwe at the end of 1993, or the beginning of 1994, and we all rejoiced. The program's first intake was in 1994, which I missed because I hadn't registered for it. So, I had to study for the one-year, Wadzanai Diploma in Religious Education, which made me a qualified religious education teacher. In 1995, I enrolled for the University of Zimbabwe Diploma in Religious Studies, whose classes were held at Wadzanai Training Center.

When I arrived at Wadzanai Training Center in February of 1994, I was as impecunious as a church mouse. I had a few clothes and one pair of shoes. I didn't have any pocket money. The Friars had told me in no uncertain terms that they were going to pay for my tuition fees and nothing else. There were other outstanding necessities. I needed washing and bathing soap, books, and bus fare at the end of every term. I knew that getting funds for these other items would be a challenge, but I didn't want that to prevent me from taking advantage of the Friars' generosity. I had to go to Wadzanai since it provided the only flicker of light at the end of the dark tunnel of my life. Before I surrendered my future to divine providence, I had sent a list of items that were required at Wadzanai to Fr. Sean, my former novice director. He had responded by telling me to just go to Wadzanai. His response had the finality of someone who felt had no responsibility for purchasing those items for me. He was right. I knew that I was pushing my luck too hard. I accepted the risk and went to Wadzanai.

In my first year, life wasn't easy at all. Whenever I wanted to wash my clothes, I would go to the laundry looking for the small pieces of soap thrown away by other students. At times, I was lucky to find a few pieces that I would use for laundry and bathing, and at other times, not. There were days when I saw larger fragments of laundry soap, but I couldn't take those because of the fear that their owners could just have forgotten them, and that they would come back looking for them. For me, picking up such big pieces would be stealing, and I wasn't a thief. My conscience wouldn't allow me to steal. I only went for the smaller portions, which I was sure had been disposed of by their owners. It worked. As I picked those disposed of pieces of soap, of course, secretly, lest someone saw me and laughed at me, I still could hear the ubiquitous voice of my mother saying, "Don't take anything that doesn't belong to you. Don't pick up anything that isn't yours." My mother would forgive me for anything, but not for picking up anything that wasn't mine. Yes, I was picking these pieces from the trash can, but for my mother, that would be picking up something that didn't belong to me. For her, that would be stealing. If you knew my mother you would understand that my fear was justified.

The Bus Fare

I survived throughout the term like that. Just when I thought that I had won the battle for survival, another challenge came at the end of the first term. I needed bus fare to go back home for the long vacation. I wrote a letter to Brother Peter, who was responsible for my tuition fees. He drove all the way from Chivhu to Harare to bring me some money, but not without chastising me first. It was a bag of coins that he claimed had been obtained by his postulants from their vegetable sales at Saint Francis of Assisi Postulancy. I could tell from his countenance that he was upset because I had asked for bus fare. The moment he invited me for a walk, I knew that all hell would break loose. He sternly reminded me that he would be responsible for my tuition fees only, and nothing else. I already knew that. He also said that if I wasn't capable of raising my own pocket money, then, I was free to drop out of Wadzanai Training Center. This conversation was very painful to me. At the end of the discussion, I wanted to reject the coins and keep my dignity, but it wasn't time for pride. My humble upbringing had taught me how to swallow my pride if necessity demanded it. I accepted the money because I needed it.

What pained me most was the fact that he reminded me that if I couldn't afford to take care of my other needs, I was free to drop out of Wadzanai. Some of you may have been involved in situations where someone pretends to give you other options, and you know that neither of them is actually a feasible option. Have you been asked questions such as: "If you are not happy here, why don't you leave?" If you don't trust me, why don't you divorce me?" If you don't like school, why don't you drop out?" If you don't like my food, why do you eat it?" In most cases, such statements are intended to make the listener feel helpless and valueless. This kind of talk is designed to coerce the one being addressed to accept any sort of treatment or advice from the speaker. Brother Peter knew that I couldn't drop out of the program because that was the only hope for a better future that I had. My life depended on staying put.

Brother Peter, being the generous person he was, might have wanted me to realize that there were worse challenges that awaited me at home than not having bus fare. I knew that he was right to remind me that the Franciscans had no obligation to take care of all my needs at Wadzanai. I had no reason to continue bothering them. What they offered me, was out of their magnanimity. Later, I thanked Brother Peter for that conversation because it forced me to think. I had no reason to complain about that reminder because of all the Franciscan religious life drop-outs, perhaps I was the only one who had received educational, financial assistance from the Friars.

Time flew. The second term came, and again the school vacation was fast approaching. Soon, I would need bus fare to go back home. This time, I was confident that I wouldn't bother the Friars. Once beaten, twice shy. Have you ever asked for a favor, which was either denied, or granted, and it made you feel really embarrassed for having asked for it in the first place? That is how I felt when I asked for bus fare from the Friars at the end of the first term of 1994, and was reprimanded for that. I was still ashamed of myself. I could have shared my predicament with Sr. Perpetua, but I couldn't do that. I didn't want to be shamed again. As I reflect on it now, I am pretty confident that Sr. Perpetua could have assisted me with some pocket money and bus fare if I had asked, but I didn't. Although Sr. Perpetua was a nun, she was well connected with influential and wealthy donors and benefactors, who would be willing to help. But, I wasn't going to beg. I wasn't going to make myself vulnerable again.

There were also other good people I could have asked for assistance, but whenever I felt that I had gathered enough energy to ask, I would hear Brother Peter's gentle voice saying to me. "John, if you can't afford to do those small things for yourself, please, go home. Don't bother other people who have no obligation to be generous to you. The food and board that we pay for you cost a fortune." At some point, I shared my predicament with one of the students who was a Redemptorist seminarian doing spiritual formation at Wadzanai Training Center. The sharing wasn't intended to ask him for anything. But, as my friend, I felt that I needed to share my story with him. I think that he felt concerned about me, and shared my challenges with his superior, who lived at Alphonsus at Tafara.

On a Monday morning, after my friend had come back from the weekend at Tafara, as he always did, he handed me an envelope. I opened it without any idea as to what it contained, and I froze upon seeing its contents. It contained some money and a note that said that it was money for my bus fare. The letter also included the name of the donor. I thanked the bearer of the gift and went into my room, closed the shatters, and cried. I really don't know why I cried, but I did, perhaps for a good one hour. As I look back at the incident now, I think that I really felt ashamed of myself. Maybe I felt both shame and joy at the same time. The embarrassment might have come from my awareness of being a basket case, and the recalling of Brother Peter's advice. If the Franciscans had no obligation to care for me, then the Redemptorists, had no obligation even to know that I existed. The joy might have come from the fact that, at long last, I had the bus fare to go home for the vacation. Despite the sorrow that I felt, I wrote a note to the donor, accepting the gift and thanking him for offering it. I will never forget that act of generosity. His name is Fr. McAinsh, just in case, you would like to help thank him.

It was at the end of the second term, or the beginning of the third term of 1994 when we were placed in the same micro teaching group with a Holy Cross religious sister. As we continued sharing our stories, she felt pity for me, and another poor student who was on our team. She is the woman who became like a mother to me.

She gave me the washing soap that I needed. She gave me an extra blanket. Sometimes, she would buy drinks for us. The other student who hailed from Gokomere was in a worse economic situation than I. Both his father and mother had died, and he had ended up in Kwekwe, where his nephew took care of him. It was in Kwekwe, where the Mary Ward Sisters noticed his potential and decided to send him to Wadzanai Training Center where I met him for the first time. The good Holy Cross nun became like our mother. She was kind and compassionate. She was a good counselor too. Whenever we misbehaved, she gave us some useful advice. She graduated from Wadzanai at the end of 1994, but we remained because we still had two more years of schooling ahead of us.

Sister Perpetua was one of the best leaders any institution of high learning could have. She was a woman of deep spirituality too. She ran Wadzanai Training Center like a Novitiate. Everything revolved around prayer. There were Divine office prayers every morning and evening. The Morning Prayers and meditation were followed by Mass. We had two Jesuit priests who came to celebrate Mass with us. They were very lovely priests except that one of them gave very poor homilies. There were evening prayers too, which were followed by supper.

The meals were delicious, and the diet balanced. The only thing that some students complained about was the provision of cabbage in almost every meal. There was a huge vegetable garden, which the gardener never tended, to my worst annoyance. Consequently, it never produced any vegetables for the students. I had been to Saint Paul's House, where I had seen the gardener transforming everything that he touched to plants. I too had mastered his skills, but at Wadzanai, I wasn't the gardener, but a student. It wasn't until eleven years later, when I went back to Wadzanai, as a professor, I showed the same old gardener a few skills about gardening. Whether he learned anything or not, it wasn't my concern, for I only wanted to provide enough greens for our students.

At Wadzanai, Sr. Perpetua was ubiquitous. She made sure that everyone attended Mass and the prayers every day. She knew everyone by name and did her role call mentally. Since we had fixed seating places in the chapel, she could quickly identify those students who would be absent. Absconding prayers was a pernicious crime, although I don't remember anyone being penalized for it. It may be that nobody absconded. Her presence was never missed in the chapel. She too was in charge of the dining hall. Her table was set up in a position where she could see everyone. She never hesitated to call gormandizers to order. She too was responsible for driving the professors to and from both Chishawasha Seminary and the University of Zimbabwe. She also taught two English language classes. She was an excellent teacher.

Sr. Perpetua was responsible for almost every facet of the Wadzanai life. No one could imagine Wadzanai without Sr. Perpetua. But, she did all with love and compassion. I can't really tell if I liked her or not very much at the time. It was after graduating from Wadzanai when I started appreciating the sacrifices that Sr. Perpetua made for all of us. Sooner, I realized that she was one of the most caring nuns that I had ever met. She remains one of my heroes. I firmly believe that she is now enjoying the fruits of her toils in Heaven, together with all other good people, who have gone before us.

At some point during my stay at Wadzanai, Sr. Perpetua went to Ireland on vacation, and she left Sr. Monica Taggart in charge of the running of Wadzanai. Sr. Monica had just arrived at Wadzanai from South Africa and belonged to a different congregation. She was in her 70s. I still don't know why she came to Wadzanai at that particular time. Other Presentation sisters could have replaced Sr. Perpetua, during her absence, but the Good Lord brought Sr. Monica. She was a very kind nun and very different from Sr. Perpetua. For the first time in my life, I received birthday gifts in the form of a Rolex watch and some money from Sr. Monica. She told me that she had bought the watch in the Comoros Islands, for her domestic employee. Unfortunately, when she arrived back in South Africa, her employee had died, and she kept the watch, which became my first birthday gift as far as I remember.

Washing Glasses at Keg and Sable

When I had an opportunity to share my story with Sr. Monica, I told her that I needed a part-time job, and wanted to know if she knew anyone who could assist me secure it. Yes, she knew somebody and was willing to introduce me to him. Together, we walked to Sam Levi Village, and she told the manager of a particular restaurant and bar called Keg and Sable, that I needed a part-time job. I got the job as a beverage glass cleaner. The manager told me that if I wanted, I could start working on that particular day, which I did. My working hours started at 8:00 pm and ended at 12:00 am, during weekends only. That job made me self-sufficient. It restored my dignity and confidence. It brought back my trust in God and humankind.

From that time onwards, I could buy my own soap and clothes. I got myself a good pair of shoes and socks. I bought five pairs of underwear, for up until then, I had relied on one pair that had seen better days. I purchased counter books in which to write notes. Sr. Monica also secured for me a summer job with some paper company in Harare. Some of my readers might want to know why I didn't think of getting a job, in the first place. Jobs were scarce in Zimbabwe at that time. Many people were looking for jobs, and couldn't find them. It was almost impossible for a student to find a part-time job at that time. Sr. Monica knew the two managers of the restaurant. They were white South Africans. Sr. Monica, being a white South African herself, effortlessly got the job for me. I will forever be grateful to Sr. Monica. She changed my fortunes. She transformed me from a soap scavenger to a wage earner. She enabled me to taste the sweetness of "eating" the fruits of my own sweat.

Sr. Monica wasn't meant to live at Wadzanai forever. She left Wadzanai as soon as Sr. Perpetua came back from Ireland. We kept in touch for a couple of months after she returned to South Africa. Eventually, we lost contact, but I hope to meet her again in Heaven or the world of the ancestors. I want to thank her for restoring my humanity, which poverty had stolen from me. Of course, I thanked her many times, but I never felt that I had appreciated her enough. One day before she left, a small party was thrown to bid her farewell. I left the party prematurely because Sr. Monica cried, and if I had stayed, I would have cried too, as if the party was held for me.

If you have never lived on handouts, you may not know how it feels to accept a donation. It humbles. It humiliates. It degrades. It dehumanizes. It embarrasses. And it shames. Human beings have pride and self-esteem. They want to be self-sufficient. They only accept handouts because they have no other way of supporting themselves, or they have managed to kill their sanity and consciences. No sane and able-bodied human being may choose to live off of charity if he or she can find a job, from which to earn a reasonable wage. What makes one ask for or accept handouts is the lack of prospective employers or friends who know influential people. I don't subscribe to the notion that any reasonable and able-bodied person, given the option of living on charity and getting a job, would opt for the former.

I met lots of good people at Wadzanai. There was Jacob who came from Kwekwe, and I have already said a few things about him. I am told he passed away when he was teaching in Banket. Our friendship was short-lived because, at the beginning of 1995, Jacob couldn't proceed to register for the University of Zimbabwe diploma in Religious Studies because he hadn't passed his English language. He fell behind us by one year and found new friends among his new classmates. There was Andrew Matsure from Mutare, a dedicated church music singer, and drummer. He too had a very caring and kind heart. Andrew was someone people could easily count on. Later, at the University of Zimbabwe, he actually spent a full night taking care of me when I fell sick.

There was Kenias Sibongo Ngwenya, a diocesan seminarian from Swaziland. He was a very generous and kind man. He gave me some clothes and writing books at a time when I couldn't afford to buy them myself. He later died in Swaziland after being ordained a Catholic priest. There were many other students that I met at Wadzanai who assisted me in one way or the other. At the end of 1996, I graduated from Wadzanai Training Center with a Diploma in Religious Education, and the University of Zimbabwe Diploma in Religious Studies. I taught briefly at Muzinda Secondary School in Zaka before I was accepted by the University of Zimbabwe to study for a Bachelor of Arts (Honors) in Religious Studies. I had one year of studies exempted from the three-year program because my diploma grades were excellent.

At the University of Zimbabwe

Life is full of miracles and surprises. Before coming to Wadzanai, I had never dreamt of studying at the University of Zimbabwe. Many students of my economic status never had such misleading dreams. It wasn't because I had no ambitions, but because I was realistic. It wasn't that I was less gifted academically, but because it took more than academic giftedness to study at UZ, as it was popularly known. In fact, I was more talented than many of the students who had found their way to the University of Zimbabwe. The university was a place that we never talked about at my high school. The University of Zimbabwe was the dream of students who were privileged to study at boarding schools, not Upper Tops. Only parents who could afford to pay the exorbitant school fees could send their children to such schools. Boarding schools had better infrastructure, more qualified teachers, and more learning resources. They also recruited brighter students. At that time, only boarding schools and a few wealthy private schools offered advanced level studies, which were a requirement to get a place at the university.

UZ considered its Diploma in Religious Studies, higher than Advanced Level studies. But, the diploma limited our program options to religious studies only. At Wadzanai, I also had an opportunity to study Advanced Level Divinity, although it wasn't a requirement for me to get into UZ. Being accepted by UZ was a big blessing at that time for anyone. In fact, UZ was one of the least expensive universities in the world, yet had high academic standards. UZ students were offered lucrative grants by the government. Food and accommodation were inexpensive. The professors were excellent and well remunerated. UZ was a sacred place for most of us who had the privilege to study there. In high schools, the teachers who had graduated from UZ were like holy cows. Every student respected them. There were very few universities in the country at that time. The National University of Science and Technology (NUST) was still in its infancy, and many students shunned it because it wasn't as renowned as UZ.

So, in 1997 I went to UZ. Of course, I had been an official student of UZ since 1995, when I registered for the Diploma in Religious Studies, while still at Wadzanai. However, UZ students matriculating at associate colleges didn't qualify for the government grant. Life at UZ was adventurous. Once in a while, the students provoked the wrath of the riot police, which in turn heavy-handedly descended upon them. I smelled tear gas for the first time. I enjoyed the moments when we marched along Second Street, now Sam Nujoma, while chanting revolutionary songs, and demanding every motorist to blow his horn for us. It was at a time when UZ students thought that there was nobody else, who was as educated and intelligent as they were. Some erroneously felt that they were above the law, and they could insult any person without being held responsible. To be a NABA/NASA (men or women not affiliated with UZ) was like a crime. It didn't matter whether one had a good job or not, as long as he was a NABA, he was considered a nobody.

At UZ there were politics of academic programs. Those students who were studying for the Bachelor of Medicine and Bachelor of Surgery (MBChB) (popularly known as MBICHIMBI) were considered the most intelligent and accomplished. I never knew what MBICHIMBI, as students called it, stood for. Of course, I knew that it had something to do with studying medicine. The trademark for these students was the white overcoat, which ended up misleading us into believing that every student who wore a white overcoat was a medical student. Later we came to know that many students who wore white coats weren't medical students. We had a classmate, who swore upon her grandmother's grave that if she were to fall in love with a UZ student, it would be an MBChB guy, not other mere mortals. I think she did find an MBChB admirer, who turned out to be not so good a lover. Their affair was short-lived. At least, she did try.

Commercial programs such as Accounting, Business studies, Economics, and others were second on the list of useful academic programs at UZ. I am not sure as to the position the law degree occupied. Law students would have studied Arts subjects at the Advanced level in high school, and that would have automatically made them look inferior to Science and commercial subjects students. Those who managed to enroll for the law degree had their fortunes transformed. Some of the law students were student leaders and knew how to give political adumbrations and harangues. I don't think that most students took them seriously. I envied the likes of Learnmore Judah Jongwe (May his soul rest in peace), whose handling of logic and the Queen's language was flawless.

Of course, there were other good degree programs that nobody cared to know about. At the bottom of all academic programs was the Politics and Administration (POLAD) degree. It seemed that no student would willingly get into that program. Students who got into it would have applied for other programs and would have failed to secure places to pursue the preferred programs. They would then just accept POLAD because it was better to just get into UZ than not at all. If your friends got to know that you were studying POLAD, you would be bullied. You could quickly lose your girlfriend if she found out that you were studying POLAD. Even people like us, who had gone to UZ to study the bible and theology, felt that our Bachelor of Arts (Honors) in Religious Studies was worth much more than POLAD.

We were young and mischievous. We never thought of the fact that every degree program was unique and essential. We never knew that it wasn't right to laugh at someone because of one's degree program. If all the students had enrolled in MBChB, then who would have become our teachers, accountants, pastors, and so on? We never looked at the struggles that students would have fought to come to UZ. As I perform some retrospection, I now know that getting into UZ was an achievement by itself. No wonder some students felt that the world owed them some respect for just being UZ students. Some of us thought that we could do anything without any consequences. Some students believed that they could be vulgar, mean, or even abusive, without being held accountable just because they were UZ students. That was one of the reasons that might have contributed to the heavy-handedness of the riot police whenever they were summoned to suppress students' disturbances at UZ. As soon as they arrived at UZ, the riot police were first and foremost reminded of their lack of education. They were even ridiculed for being first grade dropouts, which everyone knew wasn't correct. Of course, we believed it.

When I look at my academic journey, I now understand that I have achieved more than I am ready to accept credit for. It was no easy walk from the dirty classrooms of Mudarikwa Secondary School to the Mountain of knowledge as UZ was also called by those who loved it.

I met many wonderful people at UZ. I met wonderful professors. I got married in 1997, and we had both our kids when we were students. As to how I met my wife, it's a story for another day. Life at UZ was good. The government grant and loan that most students were entitled to were more than enough for most of us. I could pay my tuition and residence fees, food, and still, have some money to take care of my siblings' needs. UZ was still a world class college, unlike what it has become now. If things were as severe at UZ as they have become now, I wouldn't have afforded to study there. I am grateful that I had the privilege to study there. I now know that it was a privilege, not a right to be there. Many Zimbabweans wanted to be there, but their circumstances didn't allow them. When I graduated in 1999, I was equipped to teach any theological course. Indeed, I was and I am grateful to my professors.

CHAPTER 6

CHICAGO, HERE I COME

Goodbye Kutama College

Sometimes, we need some crisis that pushes us into progressive thinking, decision making, and strategic planning for our future. It is very comfortable and reasonable to accept the status quo and do nothing to improve one's life. Something that makes us uncomfortable has to take place to push us into action. We need to be reminded of the insecurity of our current position in order to decide to move on to something else. We avoid change because it involves taking risks. Most of the time, it's better to stick with the devil that we know than to engage the angel that we don't know. All my life, I had never thought of leaving Zimbabwe to pursue studies abroad. At Kutama College, everything seemed perfect. We had free water, free electricity, and free housing. The college gave us some incentives in addition to our primary salaries. I had a beautiful vegetable garden. I had excellent neighbors and friends. My kids' school was a stone's throw away from our house. The highway between Harare and Chinhoyi, via Murombedzi township, was just a block away from the schoolhouse that we occupied. The students were bright and respectful. The teaching resources were plenty.

But things changed, as they sometimes do. Some crisis happened that forced me to leave Kutama College, for Kutama Day Secondary School (KD). That experience reminded me of the dynamism of human lives. I also learned that those unpleasant life experiences transform us, for better or for worse. Outsiders may interpret change as a failure only because they don't understand the transformation that it brings to the insider's worldview. Change may force us to perform an introspection. Once our fortunes change, we are bound to see life differently. We begin to realize that the privileges that we sometimes mistake for rights may disappear just like fog. It may open us up to new blessings. When most of my colleagues at Kutama College thought that I had been dealt a grievous blow, I emerged more glorious. I fell in love with my new school, KD. The opportunity of teaching there enlarged my worldview. KD made me think beyond the high school classroom. I started thinking about pursuing advanced studies in Theology. I had just graduated from the UZ with a master's degree in Religious Studies and felt that I needed to go for a doctorate.

127

With the help of my all-weather friend, Brother Peter, I got a place to study for a Doctor of Ministry at the Catholic Theological Union (CTU), at Chicago. I was also offered the prestigious Bernardin scholarship, which covered all my tuition. As if those weren't enough blessings, I was provided food and board by the Franciscans, at Saint Peter's Church in the Loop. I never realized the extent and depth of my Chicago blessings until I came back to the USA as a permanent resident. I got to know that college education is costly here in the US. Many students graduate from college already carrying heavy loads of educational loans, yet I had everything paid for by the people of God. Ever since I acquired that knowledge, I have never ceased to thank all the people who contributed towards my studies at CTU. The Friars at Saint Peter's were very kind to me. In fact, I lived like a prince in their house. There were many priests and brothers at Saint Peter's, most of whom were very friendly and kind to me. Most assisted me in one way or the other. Yes, there are a lot of good people in this world, and the only challenge is that sometimes we never meet them. Occasionally, God opens a path that leads us to such people, and it's the people who are willing to take the risk of surrendering themselves to new beginnings who are likely to walk those paths. God has opened such ways for me on numerous occasions, and I have never been disappointed.

At the Catholic Theological Union

I arrived in Chicago at the beginning of August 2006. The Friar who had facilitated my stay at Saint Peter's welcomed me at O'Hare International Airport. On our way to downtown Chicago, I could see the foggy, tall buildings. My host kept telling me that Chicago was the third largest city in the USA and that it was so beautiful. It seemed as if he was persuading me to like Chicago, but I didn't need any persuasion to live in or like Chicago. I had already arrived, and I loved it. During that time, the economic situation had already become pathetic in Zimbabwe. Many people had gone into the diaspora and were sending money back to their relatives in Zimbabwe to build houses. They were also taking good care of their parents and siblings back home. Their extended families in Zimbabwe loved them. They were the first to know if any family member wasn't feeling well, or had died. They were respected by everyone. For me, coming to Chicago was like killing two birds with one stone— getting a higher educational qualification, and earning some money to support my family and friends in Zimbabwe. Both didn't prove to be easy to achieve, but doable.

A bedroom was ready for me when we arrived at Saint Peter's. I received a warm welcome from the Friars who were present. In my room, there was a computer. I had never owned a computer before, and my computer literacy was below basic. In fact, I didn't even know how to turn the computer on and off. In Zimbabwe, my wife had assisted me with all the typing and processing of my applications. I wasn't lucky this time—I was alone with my computer. Professors expected my essays to be typed. I had to teach myself how to type. In such times, God always sends you a suitable helper. There was a priest who gave me the hands-on skills concerning computers. He also introduced me to the world of passwords and flash discs. He gave me warm jackets. He was very kind and caring. He became like a father to me. At the end of my doctoral program, he proof-read my dissertation. Although some Friars never talked to me or seemed to care about me, I knew that they meant no harm to me, and were contributing to my welfare, financially.

About a week after arriving in Chicago, I had a significant setback—I got infected with tonsillitis. That wasn't my first time being affected, for I had suffered from tonsillitis several times back in Zimbabwe. The first time was in 1998 when I was a student at the University of Zimbabwe. My experience with the disease had taught me to seek medical attention as soon as I felt the first pangs of the symptoms. If treated with antibiotics on time, the symptoms just vanish. However, if left untreated until past some particular stage, the medicines wouldn't stop the signs, particularly the throat abscess. At that point, it has to run its course. Its course may take about a week, and it would be a time of involuntary fasting. Unfortunately, in Chicago, I didn't have medical insurance until about three weeks after my arrival. I had to wait for tonsillitis to take its natural course. I had to rely on painkilling medication and saltwater gaggling. I survived, but not without a few sleepless nights.

When school started, I had already fully recovered from tonsillitis. Soon I discovered that the American system of education was very different from the British education system through which I had matriculated in Zimbabwe. Soon, I realized that American professors had an insatiable penchant for assigning lots of readings to students. I wondered if the professors actually thought that the students would finish all that reading within the stipulated time. Each professor seemed to be oblivious to the fact that other professors had also assigned some reading passages to the same students.

This approach was very different from the British education system that I was accustomed to. Yes, there were readings at the University of Zimbabwe, but the prescribed texts were relevant to the research papers that one was required to complete within a stipulated time frame. I only read the parts of the book that were relevant to the essays that I would be writing. It was the responsibility of the professor to read as many books as possible, and then compile lectures notes for the students. At CTU, the professor wanted you to read the books that were required for the course, and he or she would act like the group facilitator. Students had to buy the prescribed books, and read the needed passages ahead of lectures. I found that approach very limiting since I would be confined to the views of only one author, without the opportunity to explore what other scholars would have written on the same topic. Eventually, I acquired the skills of reading as many books as possible. I survived.

Writing my doctoral dissertation was one of the challenges that I encountered at CTU. Although almost everything went smoothly with my supervisor, we had a few different views on how to tackle one of my dissertation chapters. When I reflect on the differences now, I understand their causes better. First, I had a critical approach to the Shona cultural practice of paying bridewealth, which my supervisor felt was too biased against and unfair to my culture. As an anthropologist, he thought that it was his responsibility to have an unconditional respect for culture. But, I wasn't an anthropologist—I was a theologian. I felt no necessity to respect those cultural practices that I felt weren't in line with the principles of the Gospel of Jesus Christ. Second, I had a casual approach to my dissertation topic, which further annoyed the learned professor. Third, I was away from my family, and I wanted to complete my dissertation as early as I could so that I could return to Zimbabwe. Fourth, my classmates, some of whom could barely speak and write English, were progressing in their writings, while I seemed to be stagnant at chapter two.

Fifth, I became so worried after asking one of the doctoral students about her progress in writing her dissertation. She was one year ahead of my class and looked like she was still working on her thesis. All hell broke loose when I asked her who her dissertation supervisor was. Instead of answering the question, she started sobbing. She told me that she wasn't going to graduate, at least with a doctorate, because the supervisor had already declared her a failure. She would be awarded a Master of Arts degree as an acknowledgment that she had completed her doctoral coursework. She shared with me that she had never failed an exam throughout her academic life. She had been to many different universities and had always passed with flying colors. The thought of going back to Africa, without the doctorate seemed to traumatize her.

After a lengthy discussion, she then asked me, "Who is your supervisor?" I told her, and she looked me in the eyes, and said, "That's the same professor?" My heart stopped beating for a moment. I was completely disheartened and discouraged. I tried to console the nun, but she seemed to have reached the breaking point. I promised that I would pray for her, but I didn't know what prayer to use for a person in her situation? Instead of praying for her, I ended up praying for myself. I imagined myself going back to Zimbabwe empty-handed. I could hear the voices of my friends back home whispering behind my back. "Don't you know John Chitakure? We were classmates at Wadzanai Training Center and UZ. He then went into teaching. He resigned, and went to Chicago for further studies, leaving his family behind. They say he came back empty-handed. He failed?" That was the kind of conversation that I imagined. That night, I didn't sleep well. The fear of failure almost paralyzed me. I felt that my supervisor was determined to commit me to the same dustbin of CTU history as he had done to the nun.

Sixth, I felt that my supervisor was changing the goalposts. He had read my proposal and was present when I defended it and said it was good. I couldn't understand why he would then turn around and ask me to change my thesis. There was no way I could change chapter two, which was the pillar of my research project, without changing all other four chapters. I felt that he was trying to find ways of expelling me from the program. I became terrified of him and highly suspicious of his comments, which seemed to contradict themselves at times.

Lastly, he had discredited Zimbabwean anthropologists that I had read. He dismissed their theories, without giving them a fair academic critique. It really hurt my feelings. Instead, he recommended some books that referred to Blacks as "savages." I must admit that the books contained useful information, but I felt that their usage of the derogatory words about Blacks was a bitter pill to swallow. The other issue was that he wrote contradictory comments on the copies of my chapter 2. He would ask me to delete something, and when I did that, he would ask me to include it. In the end, I had three copies of the same chapter with contradictory comments and instructions. It seemed that I couldn't go past chapter 2. When I requested him to look at my other chapters while I continued working on my chapter 2, he refused. To cut a long story short, we eventually came to an agreement that involved the director of the doctoral program. Things worked out pretty well, and my supervisor capped me when I graduated. I still have tremendous respect for him, and still think that he is one of the best professors that I have ever encountered.

It wasn't until eight years after when I started revising the dissertation for publication that I discovered that most of my supervisor's suggestions for my chapter 2 were relevant and helpful. I didn't listen to some of them because I was so scared that he would delay my graduation, or even expel me from the program. The criticism was also offered in a manner that wasn't quite charitable. Can you imagine, how it feels to resign from one's job, leave one's family, go abroad for further studies, then come back two or three years later, empty-handed.

As I think of it now, I realize that I came out of the challenges with some lessons. I got to learn that writing a doctoral dissertation was more political than it was an academic endeavor. The politics start with the choice of a supervisor. One has to do some background research of the prospective supervisor before settling on one. I failed to do my research before choosing my supervisor, as some of my classmates blamed me later. I also learned that at times, it's not the most intelligent professor who makes a better doctoral dissertation supervisor, but the one with a kind heart. I am not implying that my supervisor wasn't sympathetic, he was, in his own way. I think that he didn't know how his comments were causing more confusion than clarity. It was partly my fault because I didn't let him know. I didn't try. I thought that he was too rigid and too learned to listen to my side of the story. I might have been wrong. He had impressed me in class, and I thought that he would make a good supervisor. Little did I know that he would require the same perfectionism from me. Anyway, I survived, and I have read every book that he has written. He is a brilliant writer.

The other challenge in Chicago was that of missing my family. Before I went to Chicago, I never thought that it would be so difficult to live away from my family. The kids were well taken care of. My wife was working and providing for the kids. I had caring friends who assisted in one way or the other. But, being absent from home for two years wasn't ideal. Of course, I visited home after a year, but still, that wasn't good enough. Thanks to technology, my wife and I talked on the phone daily. We both understood that the people who make it in life were those who were ready to sacrifice something in the process. We knew what we were getting ourselves into, right from the beginning of my application process, but that wasn't good enough to cushion us from the realities of living continents apart.

Working in the CTU Cafeteria

At CTU, I worked in the cafeteria. Soon I earned respect and trust of my supervisors. They appreciated my hardworking, dependability, and humility. I was highly inspired by their appreciation. It feels good to arrive at your workplace, to find your colleagues waiting for you, and thanking you for reporting for duty. Most students at CTU didn't know that I was a doctoral student. Most of them didn't expect a doctoral student to work in the cafeteria. I remember one of my professors asking me how it felt to work in the cafeteria, and at times, waiting on my fellow classmates. I told him that I had no problem with that as long as my family back home had enough to eat. Every two weeks, I sent some money home, which my wife put to good use. Working in the cafeteria, though sometimes despised, had its own advantages. I was never short of the twenty hours per week, which I could work as a student. I also learned how to cook and clean kitchen utensils.

It was in that cafeteria where I learned that sometimes we conquer hatred by love. One day, the director told me that one of the full-time employees had been saying horrible things about me behind my back. He said that he didn't believe what she had told him because he trusted me. I knew that she had lied because I had done nothing wrong. At least, I couldn't think of having done anything unethical. When I heard that I knew that my days in the cafeteria were numbered. The same employee had caused the firing of several student employees from the cafeteria. I started thinking about how to appease, or challenge her.

At first, I thought of confronting her about her backbiting but decided against it because confrontation could easily backfire. She could easily fabricate more lies, and that could cost me my job and reputation. For a week, I was angry with her, and couldn't look her in the eyes. I guess she knew that the supervisor had told me about her backbiting. Then, I decided to approach the issue differently. I thought of hypocrisy, and it worked.

On that particular day, I arrived at work a couple of hours before the backbiting worker. When she did come, I smiled and welcomed her with a hug. I had never hugged her before. I told her that I was so happy that she had reported for work on that day, for I had been lonely. I said that I appreciated her kindness and care and that it was a privilege to have a workmate like her. I asked her if there was some kitchen chore that she wanted me to do before I continued with what I had been doing. Of course, at the time, I didn't mean any of the things that I said about her. But, it worked. She froze and blinked a couple of times before she said anything, or thank me. She might have sensed that I didn't mean it, but she decided to take the risk. She smiled and thanked me.

Both of us were transformed. She started treating me with respect. She felt safe enough to share with me about her family. I discovered that she was as human as most of us. She had her blessings and challenges. She had her strengths and weaknesses. In fact, we became friends. All the things that I had said to her without meaning them became real. I must confess that I don't know if it's her or I who changed. It could be that both of us were transformed. There is power in showing love even to one's enemies. Although we may conquer by fighting, it is true that at times, all that we need is an undeserved offering of love. Sometimes we focus too much on changing the other person without convincing ourselves that we also need to change. I changed my perception of my fellow employee, and it enabled her to show her vulnerabilities and humane side. I worked in the cafeteria until I graduated from CTU. The full-time staff was sad to see me going. I missed them very much.

Optional Practical Training

Graduation day came. I was happy to graduate, but the future was still bleak. I had applied for Optional Practical Training, a year in which I could work in the USA before going back home, and it was granted. I had started applying for jobs in Chicago as soon as January 2008. Soon, I discovered that it wasn't easy to get a job. I went to three job interviews and had been rejected by all. Sooner, I realized that I was just wasting my energy because no one was going to offer me a job, at least, within the time frame in which I needed it. I then decided to go back to Zimbabwe, where my family was. At that time, things were hard in Zimbabwe, but I trusted divine providence. I knew that the God who had brought me that far, wouldn't forsake me.

I arrived in Zimbabwe in May of 2008, at the height of the inflation craziness. The Reserve Bank of Zimbabwe was printing money and bearer checks, all the time. There were acute shortages of commodities. Some people who worked in the rural areas had stopped coming to town for their salaries because, by the time they got some money from the bank, it wouldn't be enough for their bus fare back to their workplaces. I couldn't understand the Zimbabwe dollar denominations, which at that point had more than 12 digits. People talked about trillion-dollar notes. There were endless queues everywhere. Whenever people saw a few people waiting in a line, they would just join the line without knowing what they would be queuing for. Things were bad. The shops were empty. I started thinking about the USA. I wanted to go back, but I knew that it was impossible. I felt that the situation pained me more because I knew that life could be better. I had lived in the USA. I felt that people could be happier if appropriate economic policies were enacted. Eventually, I got into the tune of things. We were lucky because I had made connections in the USA. My friends kept sending us some money, and we survived. We even managed to take care of our extended families, friends, and neighbors. There is power in friendship.

I then got jobs as a part-time faculty at several theological institutions in Harare. I got enough wages to keep us going. After three years of part-time teaching, I got a two-year teaching contract at Wadzanai Training Center. My wife was doing very well at the new company that she had joined. Soon, we bought our first car, a Toyota Corsa that had known better owners and days. We loved it, and it faithfully performed the work for which we had bought it. It was totaled after an accident. We then bought a Toyota Raum. By that time, we had already moved into our new home at Saint Georges Park, near Old Snake Park. We were happy, but we knew that there was no future for our children in Zimbabwe. The economy of the country wasn't getting any better. We had to do something about the future of the kids. We had to leave the country.

Now looking back at my experiences in Chicago and CTU, I am grateful that I was privileged to study there. CTU was a beautiful school full of positive energy. The professors were humble, professional, brilliant, and friendly. It took me some time to be able to address professors by their first names. Most of those professors were also priests, or nuns, which made it extremely hard for me to use their first names. In Zimbabwe, you don't address your professor or priest by his first name unless you are related. Of course, I wasn't obliged to do that but I just felt that I needed to do what other students were doing. I arrived at CTU at the time when they had just moved the classes to the magnificent new building across the street. It was beautiful. In addition, CTU students were very caring. There was that spirit of respect, community, and togetherness that resided in the place. It was just like one big family. Moreover, the CTU library was so rich that I found books about the Zimbabwean culture that I had never seen or heard of before. I loved CTU.

CHAPTER 7

SAN ANTONIO, TEXAS

The Diversity Visa

I heard about the USA Diversity Visa Lottery from a Zimbabwean friend who had migrated to Australia in 2008. Although I had studied in the USA, I had never heard about it. That piece of information could have escaped me because I never thought of leaving my native country to resettle elsewhere. I went to Chicago, acquired the qualification for which I studied, and went back home to Zimbabwe. I still hoped that the Zimbabwean economy would improve. But, when I arrived back home in 2008, I was disillusioned by the state of the economy and the astronomical cost of living. I regretted my failure to try to prolong my stay in the USA, after my studies. I shared my anguish with my friend, who then told me about the Diversity Visa.

In October 2010, I played the lottery, and the results came out in May 2011. I wasn't one of the lucky winners. I wasn't disappointed by the results because I hadn't expected to win. Then, a miracle happened. About a week after the release of the draw results, I received an email that said that the results had been canceled because of some irregularity that had happened during the random computer draw. A new draw would be done within a couple of weeks. Although the news gave me another opportunity of winning the lottery, I empathized with the pseudo winners. Of course, I wouldn't want to win a ticket to heaven, which would be canceled within a week. There was no guarantee that those who had won the first draw would win the second draw again.

The results of the second draw came out, and my name was among those the computer had randomly chosen to get the visa. It was my first time playing the lottery, and I won. In 2008, I had left Chicago somewhat begrudgingly because of my failure to get a one-year job. This time I was going back to the USA. Not alone, but with my family. As a Christian, I saw nothing short of God's intervention in that event. I never thought of the ancestors because I felt that they wouldn't be happy about my leaving my native country to resettle in a foreign land. As I reflect on the event now, I can't rule out the involvement of the ancestors. They might have wanted me to come to the USA so that I could take care of my extended family back home in Zimbabwe. I also got another sign from the ancestors in 2014, when we bought our home in San Antonio. One day, as I was inspecting the backyard, I noticed some familiar plant. I plucked its leaves and smelled them. Bingo! It was *nyevhe*. It was the vegetable of the ancestors, growing here in San Antonio. *Nyevhe* is the most popular indigenous vegetable in Zimbabwe. I have every reason to believe that our ancestors genuinely wanted us to be here. This was a brand-new home, in which nobody had lived, yet God and the ancestors provided *nyevhe* for us.

Challenges of Migrating

Everything has its blessings and sacrifices. The winning of the green card came with its challenges. There were lots of paperwork and medical examinations to be done. Also, we had to attend visa interviews at the USA Embassy in Harare. It was a long process. My mind and heart were divided. My mind wanted to come to the USA for the sake of the children. I knew that it would be a lot easier for them to be integrated into a new culture than it would be for us adults. Finding a job would be another difficulty. People don't just give jobs to strangers. Making new friends would also be difficult. I was very realistic about the anticipated challenges and I shared them with my family. In Zimbabwe, my wife and I had good jobs. We had a house. We were responsible for the care of our relatives. Our children were in a boarding school (Saint Francis of Assisi, Chivhu). Those weren't mean achievements for us. We had just bought a beautiful car—a Toyota Raum, which was as good as new. We would sacrifice a lot by migrating to the USA. When I tell people that we came to the USA reluctantly, some don't quite believe me. They can't conceive of anyone, who comes to the USA, reluctantly. If we had nothing to lose in the process, yes, we wouldn't have hesitated to cross over. But we had a life in Zimbabwe, and it would be hard to leave everything and start all over.

What then forced us to conquer our fears? We knew that there was no future for our children in Zimbabwe. Our children could inherit our house and car, but they couldn't inherit our jobs. They could go to good schools, and get a plethora of academic achievements, but they wouldn't get jobs in Zimbabwe. We had to make a sacrifice for the children. The USA was a God-given opportunity for our boys' future. That's what most parents do. They make sacrifices for the sake of their kids. Furthermore, coming to the USA would give my wife a chance to see the USA. I wasn't going to be selfish. When we finally decided to come to the USA, we were glad that we did. Everyone that we shared the news with was glad for us. Some even envied us. They didn't know the battle of indecision that we were experiencing. For most Zimbabweans, winning a USA green card is tantamount to getting a ticket to heaven. But I had been to the USA before, and I knew that the USA wasn't heaven.

Like any other place, it had its own blessings and challenges. For me, the challenges far outweighed the blessings.

I also knew about the culture shock. I knew about the homesickness. I knew a little bit about the racism. I was sure that it would be tough for me to find a job considering my sphere of expertise. I am a teacher of theology, and anybody in the USA can teach theology. Although I am a qualified high school teacher, I knew that the USA had its own system of teacher training and accreditation. I was aware that it would be difficult for me to find a job as a catechist in the Roman Catholic Church, not because I wasn't qualified for the job, but because there were so many of us chasing after few posts. I knew that being a stranger wasn't an easy thing for anyone anywhere. I didn't want my family and me to experience the vulnerabilities of being strangers. I got my Diversity Visa in February of 2012 but remained undecided until May of the same year. My mind convinced me that it would be beneficial to come to the USA, yet my heart told me not to. Eventually, my head won the battle over my heart. I decided to come. My family got their visas in May and were to follow me later.

It's not cheap to migrate to any country. We were lucky because we had saved some money. We could afford to pay for our physical medical check-up and immunizations. We could buy our own air tickets. We also had some money that could keep us going for about five months in the USA. We were lucky because we had friends in Chicago and San Antonio. We were offered support by friends from both cities. The friends who offered to assist us were some of the friends that had stood with us through thick and thin. We decided to come through San Antonio, on our way to Chicago. We never got to Chicago until December 2016 when we went there as tourists because we had fallen in love with San Antonio and its warm-hearted people. On the 2nd of June 2012, I arrived at George Bush Intercontinental Airport at Houston, from where I would take the Greyhound bus to San Antonio. I missed my bus because the immigration officers delayed other immigrants and I for more than two hours. I never got to know what was happening because no explanation was offered. After about two hours of standing in the line, my papers were finally processed, and I was happy that I was granted entry into the USA. My family followed in August of the same year.

Our San Antonio friend was prepared for our arrival. She picked me up from downtown San Antonio. She had reserved her back house for my family. That backhouse became our house from that time up to May of the following year. After a couple of sleepless nights in the backhouse, I discovered that my lack of sleep was caused by the blood-sucking bed bugs *(sikidzi)*. I could have identified my vampirish tormentors earlier if I had guessed that there were bed bugs in heaven. I had a rude awakening when one night I felt the bugs sucking my bitter African blood. I woke up, and to my worst horror, the vampirish creatures were all over my bed, feasting on me. My friend acted swiftly and efficiently. She had the house fumigated, and the blood-sucking insects were wiped out. It was very embarrassing to share this story with anybody from Zimbabwe because nobody expected bed bugs in America. Of course, there were more surprises to follow.

The Hunt for a Job

The hunt for a job started. I got frustrated right from the beginning. I had to apply for jobs online, which wasn't very difficult to do. However, the application systems wouldn't accept the addresses and phone numbers of my hometown, high school, and colleges. The online application systems also out-rightly rejected my reference writers' addresses and phone numbers. So, initially, I never completed and submitted an application form. I would spend about two hours working on an application, which wouldn't go through when I tried to submit it. That was very frustrating. It looked like the system was programmed to discriminate against me. It prevented me from presenting my case and being heard by prospective employers. I was technically disqualified before I even started the application process. Of course, I knew that submitting one's online application was only the initial part of the hiring process, employers could still discriminate against me in the subsequent stages if they wanted to. But, my failure to even get started made me hopeless. Have you been in that place where you know that all odds are against you? That's where I was.

But I was determined. I wasn't going to allow the discriminatory system to prevent me from pleading my case. I thought of hitting the pavement in search of a job. I visited some big grocery stores and fast food outlets in San Antonio, to plead my case with the managers. Some managers refused to even talk with me. I guess they just looked at me from their office monitors and condemned me. I was told that they were busy, which might have been correct. Other managers agreed to come down to hear my story, but would then contemptuously dismiss me.

"Go and apply online. That's our company's policy, and we aren't going to change it just for you. Who do you think you are?" One of the managers bellowed at me.

I could have said, "I am one of the dreamers from across the oceans. I need a job to provide for my family and relatives just like you do." But, I never dared to argue my case. I felt dehumanized. I felt embarrassed. What pained me most was the fact that, they had the jobs that I could perform, perhaps better than any other employee. And I needed a job. I am a Zimbabwean, and I can do manual work. If anyone wanted to know, they could have asked my former supervisor at the Catholic Theological Union cafeteria where I had worked for two years. I felt dehumanized because I had left five jobs in Zimbabwe. In fact, I hadn't yet resigned from my full-time position at one of my numerous working places. Yet, here in Texas, nobody wanted to assist me in processing just an application.

"Please, don't come back again. We will contact you after we receive your online application. Goodbye." One of the managers dismissed me. He looked at me as if he was about to vomit. I don't begrudge him for what he said because he was trying to be helpful and polite. Now, five years down the line, I still see that manager whenever I go shopping at the same store. Yes, we buy our suplies and food from that grocery store. Some of the money from my purchases contribute towards his fat salary. Of course, he doesn't even remember me. I don't expect him to recognize me. He forgot about me as soon as I left the shop. I didn't. I still remember him. Not with anger. Not with bitterness. But with sadness. A life of privilege can easily blind us from seeing the plight in another person's eyes. I don't understand how he missed my life story written all over my countenance. I guess he never looked at me, although he seemed like he did. I couldn't understand why he dismissed me like that. I needed a job, not a part of his salary. He had the position that I could perform. They were hiring. It wasn't a secret because the information was all over the internet and their billboards. I pitied him because he had deprived himself of a damn good worker.

In one of the stores, they had a notice that said that they were recruiting employees, and applications could be completed in the store. I thought that it could be my lucky day. I felt that someone in the store was going to assist me. I went to the corner where they had machines that looked like massive computers, and I started reading the instructions on how to process my online application. Before I even struck a single key, all hell broke loose. The manager came to me fuming. "Who are you?" He wanted to know.

"I am John," I responded.

"What do you want?" He demanded to know.

"I would like to process my online job application. I haven't started because I am still reading the instructions. Would you please, assist me?" I was innocent.

"We have no jobs." He fumed.

"But, that notice says that you are hiring?" I pointed at the big notice on the wall of the store.

"I am the manager, and we don't have jobs here. Please, leave. Go." Then my Mexican American friend who had gone to the other part of the store came to my aid.

"He is good. He is with me." She told him. He was appeased. He just walked away, leaving us speechless. My friend grabbed me by the hand, and we unceremoniously departed the store. She then gave me a thorough and useful lecture on race relationships in the USA. She told me that since I was Black, the manager might have thought that I was a robber. I was shocked. Yes, I had read about racism in colonial Zimbabwe. I had read about apartheid in South Africa. It sounded terrible, but, it's different when you experience the things that you have read in books and newspapers. My eyes were opened and I regretted my naivety. I never thought that there were such glaring racial stereotypes in the USA. The idea that my family and I would be considered second-class citizens in the USA was a bitter pill to swallow.

But I wasn't going to give up. I learned a gimmick of persuading the online application system to accept my application. I supplied the phone numbers and area codes that the employment application system took although they didn't exist. I replaced all my Zimbabwean referees by Americans, some of whom I had met only once. The system was fooled, but not the employers. Soon the employers started responding to my applications. They politely thanked me for my interest in their companies and the advertised job posts but regretted that the amount of applications that they had received had overwhelmed them, and they had chosen other applicants. However, they encouraged me to apply for additional suitable positions in the same companies. Soon, I realized that most of the responses that I received were almost similar. It's like the human resource managers were copying each other. All of them were very polite but unyielding. I knew that getting any kind of job in San Antonio was almost impossible. What frustrated me most was that the employers that would have rejected me continued to look for employees for the same posts. My friend was right. My fears of coming to the USA were being confirmed.

I started resenting one of the questions that I had encountered in most, if not all, the online job applications. It's a question concerning one's race, which all the employers said was optional, and the answer wouldn't be used to deny any applicant the job. I started feeling that the question was intended to identify my race for segregation purposes. I suspected that the moment I identified myself as Black African, my application form would be discarded. I could just leave that part blank since it was optional, but that would be a huge signal that I wasn't white. If the system favored white citizens (I later learned that they call it, "white privilege"), as I suspected, I don't imagine any white job applicant leaving that question blank. Either filling out the requirement or ignoring it would be detrimental to my success. Moreover, my last name could quickly tell that I wasn't white. A couple of times, some employers thought that I was Japanese because of my last name. That error might have contributed to some employees calling me to find out.

One of my white friends in Chicago had an idea. He introduced me to someone, a friend of his, who I had briefly met in Ohio, in 2006. At that particular time, he was working here in San Antonio. My Chicago friend had alerted him of my arrival in San Antonio, and my need for a job. My friend explained that this man could help me since he held an influential position in the Church. I emailed him, and he came over to pick me up for lunch. As we were eating, he said something that I will never forget in my life. He enlightened me about racial politics in the USA.

"John, it will be tough for you to get a job. Do you know why?"

I said, "No."

"Because you are black. You are African. Some people here don't trust blacks. They believe that blacks are lazy. Blacks don't want to work. Blacks play the color game. You take a big risk if you employ them. If you are the supervisor, and you try to correct them about something, they accuse you of racism. Here, you can get into big trouble if someone accuses you of racism. Many employers want to stay away from that trouble. They just don't employ blacks unless they know them. Now with your heavy accent, many employers will try to stay away from you. I will try to talk to some people that I know, but I can't promise you anything. I will also talk to my manager. He might not even want to meet with you."

"But, don't get discouraged. Keep looking. These are just stereotypes if you have ever heard of them." He encouraged me.

I thanked him for being honest with me. I knew that it was a risk for him to share that information with me. I felt that he just wanted to be honest with me. I respect him for that. Whenever I share this experience with some white Americans, their first reaction is to condemn the man. "That was very wrong for him to tell you that." Some of them would say. Others don't make any comments, but I usually see the embarrassment on their faces. I later, learned that some of them denounce the man, not because what he told me was completely wrong. They condemn him for divulging the conspiracy which says, "Deal with them silently. Don't use the "N" word. Address them as "Sir" or "Madam." When you meet them, show your utmost respect. But, stay away from them in a manner that is within the laws of the land. Don't tell them that you don't like them. Don't tell them that they are lazy. Just stay away from them, within the provisions of the law." My friend violated all those unwritten regulations of racial interactions. He spilled the beans.

My reference person never came back to me, and I wasn't disappointed. I didn't expect him to come back to me. I vowed not to contact him unless he initiated it. Of course, what he told me had a chilling effect on me. Nobody wants to be prematurely judged. We all want to be given an opportunity to present our cases before being judged. Nobody wants to be condemned for the sins of others. I don't disagree that some black people are lazy, but the same is equally valid about any race. Lazy people are everywhere. I felt that it was very unfair to condemn the whole race for the sins of a few individuals. What frustrated me most was the knowledge that there was nothing I could do to change the system, and people's worldview. I felt that by deciding to come to America, I had accepted the risk of being discriminated against on account of my skin color. I had opted for the vulnerabilities that come with otherness. I had opted for the insecurities of being a stranger. I had to face the music.

I know that sometimes stereotypes are fabrications that some people create to dehumanize a group of people that they don't like. In my book, Shona Women in

Zimbabwe—A Purchased People (2016), I wrote about how some men would denounce their wives as witches to make them vulnerable and to isolate them. A witch is an evil person, who possesses secret, evil, and mysterious powers to harm others. Once somebody convinces the village that the woman in question is a witch, they may begin to hate and marginalize her. That ostracization allows the accuser to abuse her in any way, and the society won't come to the woman's aid since she is deemed evil.

The same happens in most human communities. Influential people stereotype the people that they don't like, usually, the poor and disadvantaged groups. They convince everyone that the victims are lazy, evil, dangerous, and criminals. They create fear in in their family members. Once most influential members of the society begin to believe the lies about the disadvantaged groups, the powerful can oppress, ostracize, exploit, and discriminate against the stereotyped group. No one sympathizes with them. No one tries to challenge the lies that they peddle. If the stereotyped group tries to resist the stereotypes imposed on its members, it is condemned as a group of angry people. Yes, they might be angry, but no one cares about the cause of their anger. Being angry becomes a pernicious crime. If the so-called angry people look for jobs, they aren't considered. If they ask for government aid because they have no jobs, they are condemned as lazy and good for nothing. If they run away from school because of poverty and discrimination, they are doomed as unintelligent and antisocial. If they persevere and get into colleges, they are condemned as having benefitted from affirmative action. The system will always have a way of denouncing them, whatever they do.

But, it wouldn't be fair if I didn't mention the other side of the same coin. Stereotypes are mutual. Whites are stereotyped as racist. Whatever they do or say, they are racist. The racist stereotype can be used to justify one's behavior. If I violate one of the laws of the land, and I get arrested, I condemn the cops for being racists. If I don't do my job, and the supervisor corrects me, I accuse him of racism. If I don't do my homework, and the teacher tries to discipline me, I suspect her of bigotry. I agree that some of the accusations may be true, but what is wrong is to condemn all members of a particular race because of the sin of a few. Since I don't want to be held responsible for the misdeeds of others, I shouldn't hold others accountable for someone else's misgivings.

Anyway, coming back to my story, I bumped into my reference person at his church some three years after our initial meeting. He looked at me and smiled. I am grateful that he was brave enough to share that information with me. He was right. His manager didn't want to see me. But, I wasn't deterred. I continued searching for a job. Someone told me about a place where I could register for assistance in looking for a job. I registered, and they called me after about a month because they had a job for me. I went to the outer office and waited. The recruiting officer came out from his inner office to meet me. He was a young man in a wheelchair. I introduced myself. He looked at me as if he was in great astonishment. He shook his head from side to side, most probably, involuntarily. It seemed like he was in utter disbelief. Immediately, I sensed that something was wrong.

"You know John, there should be some mistake. I didn't intend to call you. I wanted to call somebody else. This was a mistake. I am sorry. I will keep your file, and will call you when I get an appropriate job for you." That was the last time that I heard from him. I knew that he wouldn't call me. I felt that he was surprised to find out that I was African. I understand that my analysis can be wrong. I must admit that at that time, the USA racial narratives had already started shaping my experiential interpretations. Whenever I share this story with my American friends, they are quick to judge him. They also remind me that I should have reported him. They forget that most aliens feel really powerless and vulnerable in any foreign land. An alien knows very well that his credibility is far less than that of a citizen. The other challenge that every immigrant doesn't want to face is to create trouble for the citizens. After all, you aren't even sure why you are treated the way you are. In other words, you don't have the proof or evidence.

I kept applying for jobs until I got tired. Then a miracle happened. My friend knew someone who knew someone, who was willing to take the risk of offering me a part-time job. The supervisor knew someone, who also was ready to take the same chance by providing me a second part-time job. I had an interview for the second part-time job, and another miracle happened. One of the panelists had been to Zimbabwe. She had visited Zimbabwe in 1997 as a delegate at the World Council of Churches summit that was held at the University of Zimbabwe. I was doing my second year at UZ in that year, and one of my friends was an usher at that meeting. After we shared that information, I felt that she would risk by offering me the part-time teaching position. This job became one of the two part-time posts that I had in the land of the living for several years. It kept me going and gave me the hope to keep hoping. I worked hard, and I didn't disappoint her. I learned that sometimes, it takes only one person to demythologize some racial stereotype. If you are offered an opportunity to showcase your talents and skills, don't leave any grain of doubt in the minds of your employers as to how good you can perform the duties for which you were employed. That way, you may help influential people to discard the stereotypes that they have always believed to be true and to reconstruct a new narrative about others.

The Culture Shock

My family arrived in San Antonio, in August 2012, just before I started the second part-time job. I became homesick and upset. Their arrival signaled that the decision to leave Zimbabwe was final and irreversible. I was also angry that I was failing to get a full-time job. I regretted having played the Diversity Visa lottery. I wanted to go back home. We talked about this with my wife who couldn't understand why I wanted us to go back to Zimbabwe. We had lost our jobs already. We had sold our car. We had removed our kids from a prestigious boarding school. People would laugh at us. I was agitated for almost two weeks. I became nearly incapacitated to some extent. I was angry with myself and my lack of foresight. I cursed myself for acting impetuously. I lost my appetite. It felt like I was undergoing culture shock, but I still don't believe it was. I knew about culture shock. I had taught students about it. This was different. We started making plans for a possible and shameful return to Zimbabwe. Then, a miracle happened. I woke up one day, and I was feeling normal. I realized that there were decisions that couldn't be reversed so quickly. I had already decided to come to the USA. I had to face the music. We stayed.

Now, as I look back at those two weeks, I think that what I felt was an inevitable grieving period, which was necessary for my radical reorientation. It was a time for discernment. It was like coming to terms with the loss of a beloved one. I had left my beloved country. I had left my job. I had left my friends and relatives. Most of my connections to the past had figuratively died. It was a big loss for which I needed time to grieve. Moreover, I was experiencing the pangs of a new life, away from the usual environment. I had to struggle against the new challenges. That was a rebirth. And no birth is without pangs.

Two people kept me going. Our all-weather friend was very supportive. My wife still had some energy. The two registered the kids in school. Soon my wife got a job through an agent. That position gave us the relief that we needed. Of course, we still had our savings from the sale of the car. Many other people were very kind to us. Our friend stood by us. She assisted us in every possible way. She lived with her mother, a beautiful, loving, and graceful woman. She spoke Spanish and understood very little English, but I could follow almost everything that she said. She shared her life stories. Her struggles weren't very different from my own mother's battles in raising us. I came to love her like my own mother. For me, she was a mother that God provided us here in the alien land. I regret that I missed some of her inspiring stories because of my ignorance of the Spanish language. Although I didn't understand even a single Spanish word, my heart understood the crux of her stories by reading her facial expressions. She was generous too. She donated some of her precious furniture to us, some of which we still use.

Now that we have settled down in Texas, I know why it was so difficult for me to accept my new reality. We were doing alright in our country. It is easier for a person who doesn't have a job and property to migrate because he has nothing to lose. It's more difficult to start afresh if you already possess something. Now I think that we made an excellent decision to stay. My wife and I know very well that we may not achieve the American dream, but we have high hopes for our kids. We know that we may not be able to leave them millions of dollars, but we have given them a conducive environment to start a life. We sacrificed everything to start afresh for their sake. They are already in the system and learning the ropes. One thing we know for sure is that they won't be as ostracized as I was.

As I started teaching, I knew that I had to be upfront about certain things, particularly my accent. I told my students that I had an accent. It wasn't an apology, but just a statement of the facts. There was no secret about it. I forewarned them that it would be hard for some of them to understand everything that I said, initially. I allowed them to feel free to stop me whenever they didn't understand what I said and ask for clarification. I also told them that my teaching style was different from what they were used to since I was a product of the British education system.

But, I didn't hide the blessings that I was bringing to them. I told them that my most fabulous and unique gift to them was my otherness. I had new stories that they had never had before. I had experiences that they had never experienced. I promised to respect them and assist them to achieve the best that they could. I vowed to treat all the students equally and fairly. I reminded them that my tests were intended to prove that they remembered what we would have covered in class discussions rather than what they didn't remember. I promised them that by the end of the semester, their horizons would be broader than the students that were taught by American professors, for I was giving them an opportunity to see and interpret reality through extra lenses.

I fulfilled the promises. I respected them, and they reciprocated. I listened to them and they returned the favor. They shared their views, and I affirmed them. If I were to challenge some of their views, I did that with respect and love. Before the end of the semester, we had become a team. That very first class spread the news about the excellent new teacher on the block to other students. The next semester some students who enrolled in my classes told me that they had been referred to my class by my former students. Every semester, students evaluate professors, and whenever I read the feedback, I was deeply touched by what the students wrote about me. They were so kind, appreciative, truthful, and honest. They appreciated my passion, knowledge, teaching approach, and worldview. Some of them wished that the university should offer me a full-time contract.

Learning to Care for the Sick

In 2015, I decided to enroll in the clinical pastoral education at one of the local hospitals. I learned many things about myself that I wouldn't have learned if I hadn't gone through that process. I learned about the importance of identity, empathy, and acceptance. I met people who possessed empathy. People who made me feel that I was important. People who listened to me, challenged my provincial worldview, and then affirmed me. They allowed me to share my stories and listened to them as if they mattered. I also got to listen to stories that opened my eyes. I learned to draw meaning out of some stories that seemed to be insignificant. Most of them were stories of human suffering. Stories of aborted dreams. Stories of unfulfilled and abandoned hopes. Stories of unrealized dreams. Stories of our human frailty and finitude. But, amidst such stories of suffering and pain, there were rays of hope. The hope that things would be alright. The belief that even if things don't become better, there was always some blessings in them.

One of my most significant learnings was about the use of my otherness to connect with the people that I ministered to. I learned how to offer them another perspective on human suffering and the hereafter. I shared with them another understanding of human hopes for the future. Without taking anything away from their belief system, I encouraged them to look at human finitude from another angle—my angle. Those who tried received a new framework in which to understand their sickness and impending demise. I shared my stories with them, and some of them were touched and transformed. I also learned how to listen, even to the untold stories of my clients. I helped them to draw meaning from their stories, beliefs, and rituals. I termed my fear of rejection because of racial prejudices. I learned how to test my preconceived assumptions about people's motives. I discovered how to claim my space, and assert my pastoral authority, in a non-aggressive manner.

I had my challenges too. One of the problems that I will never forget was when I was on call, and one of the Intensive Care Unit nurses called me about a patient who wanted me to assist her complete a Do Not Resuscitate (DNR) form. I told the nurse that chaplains didn't do the DNR. I told her that I could assist the patient to complete the Medical Power of Attorney form the following morning if she needed one. I also said that since it was in the middle of the night it would be difficult to find the needed two witnesses. The caller said it was okay, and asked for my name, which I happily gave her.

The following morning, about 11:00 am, when I was coming from doing my rounds, I found my clinical pastoral education supervisor and clinical director waiting for me. I sensed that something was wrong when they ushered me into the director's office. The previous night's caller had reported to her director that I had refused to come to the hospital to give pastoral care to a dying client who desperately needed it. As if that wasn't damaging enough, she had also told her director that I had said to her that the patient had to wait until the following morning. I was devastated. The nurse had either fabricated the allegations or misunderstood our communication.

What pained me most was that I was in the hospital, and still awake, at the time I received the call. I only needed two minutes to get into the Intensive Care Unit and perform the things for which I was trained. The hospital provided an on-call room for the chaplains. Those chaplains who didn't want the hustle of driving at night after being called to the hospital would spend the night in that room, which had a bed and bathroom. All the time I worked at that hospital I spent my on-call nights in that room, waiting for calls. At the beginning of my shift, I always gave the hospital operator the chaplain room phone number in addition to my cell phone number that she already had by default. If I had understood what the nurse wanted me to do, I could have just walked into the room where the patient was, to minister to her. I was in the hospital. I was awake. I was waiting. I answered the call. But, I didn't understand what the nurse was talking about. Or, she didn't understand what I said. I had failed to perform the duty for which I was waiting.

I asked if the conversation could be retrieved, but unfortunately, there was no recording of it in the first place. I was also told that the caller couldn't be interrogated. I felt like my director had already taken the caller's side. I cried. I cried not because I was afraid to lose my studentship, but because I felt that there was no justice. I thought that I was held accountable for a miscommunication that involved two persons. I was upset that the other person was allowed to go Scot free. She had the privilege that her skin color and profession bestowed on her. I apologized for the miscommunication and promised that a mistake of that nature would never happen again. And it never happened again. At the end of the meeting, I felt better because both the supervisor and director didn't seem to be very anxious about the damaging report. The other factor that alleviated my anxiety was the knowledge that my CPE supervisor was an honest, empathetic, fair, and just person. In fact, he was a healer who never used his powers to heal anybody. His therapeutic energy was in the questions that he asked, and promptings that he offered, that would persuade you to heal yourself. I healed myself and forgave the nurse.

The on-call incident taught me a few things. I learned that in any given conversation between persons, misunderstandings can happen. Hence, the need by both speakers to be as clear as possible, and ask for further clarification, if need be. I realized my vulnerable position as a chaplain at my clinical site. I learned that some misunderstandings couldn't be clarified, once experienced. I also learned that in a clash between the powerful and the weaker, the latter is likely to shoulder the blame. However, the incident encouraged me to be better in my communication with the interdisciplinary team. I still don't know what was likely to happen to me if both the supervisor and director hadn't accepted my explanation of what had transpired between the caller and me. I have every reason to believe that the accusations were so grave that I could have been discontinued from the program. I survived. I moved on.

The other issue that bothered me in the hospital was the unequal treatment that I received from some members of the interdisciplinary team that included doctors, nurses, social workers, dieticians, and others. Although in theory we were supposed to be equal members of the healthcare team, I sometimes felt that some members didn't treat me as an equal. At times, I felt being disrespected and my ministry belittled. There were some medical doctors who would walk into the room in which I was praying with the patients, and wouldn't give me an opportunity to conclude my prayer. I knew how desparately some of my clients would have waited for the healer, and I wouldn't squander that opportunity. What I expected was to be given the chance to say "amen." There were some medical practitioners who never answered my greetings. But, I never stopped greeting them. I had to be extra careful not to stand in the way of other team members. Be that as it may, I had a chance to work with some wonderful nurses, doctors, social workers, and so on. I am referring to those colleagues who made me feel that I belonged to the team, and my services were valued.

Finding a Worshiping Place

For most Christian migrants, the church might be the first place where one looks for connections. But, for my family, finding a Catholic parish in which we could feel at home presented a big challenge. We tried several churches without feeling very welcome or accepted. At one of the churches, which we attended for about four months, we felt being segregated against more than anywhere else. Before the beginning of the Mass, the pastor would walk down to the pews to greet the people. Whenever he reached our seat, he always skipped it and would go to the next. In the beginning, we thought that it wasn't by design. When it happened on many other occasions, we knew that we weren't wanted. It was time to leave, and look for another parish.

We joined another parish, where I tried to connect with the pastor, to no avail. His secretary kept me on the waiting list forever. I also tried to join the Knights of Columbus, and I was tossed from one person to another until I gave up. After a year, we bought a home on the other side of the city and started attending a new parish. The parish priest was very kind to us and asked me to help in the formation of religious education volunteers. There was a problem before I even started. The priest was transferred, and the director of the Christian education didn't need my service.

We left that church after about three months and decided to stay at home. We tried other parishes including non-Catholic, but the song was the same. Eventually, we found a parish where we felt at home.

Getting a Driver's License

At some point, I needed a driver's license because we wanted to buy a car. But before I could get my license, I needed a car. My all-weather friend couldn't help me because she had moved to another town. I talked to the people that I knew, but no one was willing to loan me a car. Eventually, I got to know about a driving school that could lend me a car, but only after taking some driving classes with them. The instructor was very kind. The car was old, and it nearly failed to pass the inspection that is performed just before the test is done. That very same day, I got my license. The next morning, we bought our first car.

The 2016 USA Presidential Elections

One of the USA experiences that I found captivating was the 2016 Presidential elections, and I wouldn't have done justice to my experiences here in the USA if I didn't say something about them. These elections were unique in the sense that the contestants were diametrically opposed regarding their political ideology and gender. On the one hand, Mrs. Hillary Clinton (Democrat) was a woman, perhaps the first one to reach that stage in USA Presidential elections. She had tried before and failed. In 2008, her journey to the White House had been cut short by Mr. Barack Obama during the primaries. Mr. Barack Obama became the first African American and the 44th USA President. Things seemed different this time. Madam Hilary Clinton was poised for victory. In fact, that is what her supporters and the media unwaveringly believed. They supported her in every known way despite her alleged mishandling of her official emails when she was the Secretary of State. The media and some political analysts claimed that she had won all the presidential debates, which might have been an accurate evaluation of the proceedings.

On the other hand, there was the candidate who later became the President of the USA, Mr. Donald Trump (Republican), who some people criticized for being a political Johnny-come-lately. There was a lot of demonization and counter-demonization by both political parties. There was an unprecedented level of intolerance among both groups of supporters, particularly those who supported Mrs. Hillary Clinton. They condemned Mr. Trump's followers as racists and anti-immigrant. Mr. Trump's supporters were also accused of being intolerant of religious and cultural diversity. It seems that the Trump supporters responded by going underground. In San Antonio, it was rare to come across a person who openly claimed to support Mr. Trump during the campaign period. But I knew that they were there. Everybody did.

As an outsider and a person disallowed by the law to vote, I could listen to the arguments put forward by both candidates from a neutral point of view. That perspective almost earned me enemies among my colleagues. Some thought that since I was an immigrant, I was supposed to support Mrs. Clinton who seemed sympathetic to immigrants. Others argued that as a black person I was supposed to be a Democrat. My response always irritated some of them. I told them that I wasn't a registered voter. That, even if I were a voter I wouldn't publicly declare the candidate that I supported. That, it wasn't a given that my skin color would determine the candidate that I would vote for. I said that my vote wouldn't be for free. I would give it to the presidential candidate whose message appealed to me, not because of what other people thought or did. For me, that's the heart of democracy; being able to freely choose the leader of my country. Some of my colleagues didn't like that line of argument, but a few did.

The reactions of the voters after the announcement of the election results were expected, at least by me. Some of my friends publicly cried. They were nursing deep fear, grief, and bitterness. I learned essential lessons about democracy. Democracy can be a bitter pill to swallow, particularly when your candidate loses. To some extent, some people can only be democratic as long as their candidate is winning. I also observed that some voters weren't educated about the democratic process and its consequences. If you give people an opportunity to elect their own president, then, whoever has the majority of votes should be respected. That's democracy. Some Americans, mainly, Mrs. Clinton's supporters weren't prepared for Mr. Trump's victory. They had hoped to win, and some of them had never imagined losing. When the presidential election results were announced, there was shock, denial, and panic, which eventually turned to bitterness, tinged with fear. Many weren't prepared for a loss because they hadn't anticipated losing. Some media practitioners had misled them with its erroneous polls that were in favor of Mrs. Clinton.

As an outsider, I had prepared myself for either candidate's victory. I had sensed that Mr. Trump was likely to win. On many occasions, I had forewarned my democrat colleagues to mentally prepare themselves for a possibility of Mr. Trump's win. I had advised them not to underestimate the popularity of Mr. Trump's message to some American people. Many disagreed with me. Some even castigated me for betraying the black people's cause by insinuating Mr. Trump's win and also giving them unsolicited advice.

"How dare you say Mr. Trump might win? Yes, let him win, and he will send you back to Africa." Some of them said. That is what happens when people refuse to see both sides of the coin. That is what happens if you ignore the small voices of the people who oppose you. That is what happens when you don't understand the political dynamics of your own society. The signs were there, but some voters chose to ignore them.

I guessed that Mr. Trump would win because of several reasons. First, he became the voice of many voiceless Americans who are afraid to speak their minds about racial issues, lest they become anathematized by the society. The American society can be so unforgiving to anyone who publicly makes a mistake of showing racial bigotry. They relentlessly pursue you, but that doesn't mean that the pursuers are beyond reproach. Consequently, some people denounce racism explicitly but may exercise it implicitly. What some people don't realize is that the race issue can't be resolved by silencing the people who see things differently. Silence doesn't take away the deep-rooted hate and attitudes that some people harbor in their hearts. If people with different perspectives on specific issues feel threatened, they just go underground. The better approach to dealing with racial prejudices and superiority complexes is to encourage a dialogue in which people share their views, though bigoted. Such a process allows the reframing of one's worldview through listening to different narratives. It seems Mr. Trump became the silenced Americans' prophet by speaking the things that they had always wanted to say, but couldn't because of the lack of a safe platform.

Second, some Americans innocently didn't realize that racial prejudices and discriminations were still rampant in the American society. Hence, accusing a political candidate of being intolerant of minority races wouldn't necessarily sway people's votes. Most Americans had great trust in their systems and strongly believed that they worked meticulously. They thought that when the government told the people not to discriminate against the minority groups, most people would oblige. Hence, most people believe that immigrants and members of the minority groups are treated as equals in the American society. But, there is still discrimination based on color, race, and even gender. You can only experience it if you are either the perpetrator or the victim. In some cases, the discrimination is so subtle that those who don't practice it find it hard to believe that it exists. Consequently, some people erroneously thought that since the media accused Mr. Trump of showing some racial biases, many people wouldn't vote for him. In fact, in some circles, it became scandalous to declare one's allegiance to Mr. Trump. But, that didn't deter them.

I think that Americans need to learn a few things about democracy and racial relationships from this past presidential election. First, they should learn that in a democracy, people choose the candidate that they want. That's the crux of democracy. Second, democracy compels people to respect the decision of the majority. It is about the candidate that is elected by the majority of voters, not how some voters feel about the winner. You may not like that winning candidate, but the voice of the people should be respected. At times, you are luck; your candidate wins, but at other times, your candidate doesn't win. Democracy is not a piece of cake because at times it gives you bitter herbs.

Third, the fact that some people don't openly discriminate against the minority and immigrants doesn't mean that racism is completely gone. Sweeping problems under the carpet doesn't help; we have to face them. Fourth, some voters don't publicly declare the candidate that they support, so predicting the winner may not be always accurate. Polls are good, but they should be taken with a pinch of salt. Finally, actions speak louder than words. It isn't what people say, but what they do, that matters. People may avoid derogatory terms about the other, but that doesn't mean that they respect the other person. They may not tell you the presidential candidate that they support, but that doesn't mean that they support or should support yours.

Some of you may be interested in knowing the candidate I would have elected if I were an American voter. I won't respond to that question. I will cross that bridge when I arrive there. As of now, I am satisfied with being a spectator. My responsibility is to celebrate with the winners and grieve with the vanquished. A time shall come when I won't have the pleasure to be neutral. Even then, I won't vote according to my skin color, religion, or culture, but I will follow my conscience. I won't just give away my vote in a silver platter, but the candidate has to earn it. I also won't announce my favorite candidate prematurely because I believe in changing my mind.

The Challenge of Educating Children about Racism in the USA

Racism is one of the most evaded issues in the USA. One of the challenges that my wife and I face as African parents are about how to educate our children about the racism in the American society without being biased or sowing the seeds of racial hatred in them. Most African children were born in post-colonial countries, and they don't know much about racism. Although some of them have read about racial segregation in colonial Africa, they didn't experience it. These children also have tremendous trust and respect in the equality in the American society. They unwaveringly believe that the American civil institutions can protect them from any discrimination based on race.

I teach my children that there is racism in the USA even though people don't talk about it. It's subtle but rampant. It exists in attitudes and hidden actions. I teach them that they are likely to experience racial segregation because they are black. Usually, blacks are stereotyped in the USA. That they are likely to be ill-treated because of their skin color. That they may be denied job opportunities because of their color. I tell them that many racists operate from underground. They put systems in place that will allow them to segregate blacks without being held accountable. That is the reality.

But, I also teach them that there are many Americans who aren't racist. Americans who appreciate diversity, and see the image of God in every human being. Americans who offer equal opportunities to everyone irrespective of color or creed. I know it from experience. Both my wife and I have White and Mexican American friends who treat us like their own family members. I teach them not to generalize about racism, and also not to be naïve. I encourage them to do their best in everything that they do.

I advise them to work hard, to be honest, to strictly uphold the laws of the land, and to study. I urge them to earn the trust of their employers and friends. I instruct them to maintain their identities, and at the same time being open to learning new cultures. I tell them to be proud of who they are. I tell them to respect everyone. I want them to transcend the racial divide that exists here in the USA. I want them to look at every person and see the image of God, not a black or white person. I don't want them to be enslaved by the unwarranted racial hatred of the other. I teach them not to judge people because of how they look like, but because of what they do. I teach them to love people.

CONCLUSION

There are lots of things to learn from our experiences. You shouldn't allow your life situation to hold you back. Some life situations make it hard for us to believe in ourselves. They rob us of our confidence and hope. They teach us to be pessimistic and at times, even to hate ourselves. They compel us to over romanticize our weaknesses and to affirm that we are beyond redemption. But, the people who succeed in life never stop believing in themselves, and in the power of hard work. You should continue believing in yourself. Continue to affirm and cultivate your talents. Continue to work hard.

But, for you to be able to claim your abilities, you have to identify them first. You should know the things you are good at. You can't be a jack of all trades. Nobody is. Many people get discouraged when they try new things and fail. Sometimes, it takes some time for you to identify your gifts, but don't abort the hunt. While it is noble to persist, there are times when tenacity becomes a sheer waste of time. Identify your niche. Don't bump your head on a wall that will never give in because you will end up hurting your head. Strike a balance between pessimism and optimism. It is only in imagination where life doesn't have vicissitudes. In real life, there are challenges, and you need to be prepared for them. Never be afraid to accept defeat if you believe that it is the wisest thing to do at that moment. At times, it is considered heroic to accept your limitations and concentrate on the things, which you are good at. Don't hesitate to cry when it's time to grieve.

You will meet haters who will try to discourage you from achieving your dreams. Learn something from their hatred, but don't stop aspiring to be who you are destined to be. You have heard that the bus will keep moving despite the relentless barking of the dogs. Do likewise. However, there are times when you have to take the noise of the barking dogs seriously. There is wisdom in realizing that, it's not every dog's bark that should be ignored. Learn something from what people who don't quite like you say.

In the pursuit of your dreams, make connections. Some people have the information and the kindness that can change your life situation. The only challenge you will have is finding them. Search for the right people who have the information. Don't impose yourself upon influential people because that can be your undoing. Don't sell your heart to be successful in life.

Encourage others. Wish them well. Bless them. Don't be jealous of other people's successes. Be generous. Be kind-hearted. Be considerate. Don't judge others. Life experiences have taught me that it's not good to judge people if you don't know where they have come from—the journey they have traveled and completed, the battles they have fought and won, and the struggles that still lie ahead of them. It's tempting to judge people, even those who you don't know. It feels good to sentence them and trash them like filth. You see people driving cheap cars, you judge them, yet you don't look at the odds that they have overcome to purchase those vehicles. You see single mothers, and immediately judge and trash them, yet you don't understand the abuses and challenges that they have survived, and the sacrifices they make to care for their kids.

The Political Science and Administration (POLAD) students at the UZ were stigmatized. We laughed at them. We trashed them. Yet, we never wanted to listen to the stories of their journeys. We didn't have the wisdom to read such stories from their countenances. We didn't care. What we saw in them, were failures; irredeemable failures. As I was busy despising POLAD students, some other students were doing the same to me for enrolling at UZ to study the bible and theology. I was judged and found wanting. Yet, those who judged me never knew where I had come from, or where I was headed. They didn't care about the plans that I had for the future. They had no idea about the battles that I had fought and won. The only thing that they saw in the likes of me was doom. If I knew what I know now, I could have tapped on the shoulders of the despised POLAD brother, and said, "Brother, I am happy that you are here. I celebrate that you have come this far. I respect you for not giving up. I want you to know that you are valuable. Your degree program, though different from mine, is equally important. Please, never stop dreaming."

In the early 80s, we used to despise the Mozambiquean refugees who fled to Zimbabwe to find refuge. We called them names such as Makarushu. If I knew what I know now, I would have tapped the shoulder of the Mozambiquean immigrant, and said, "Brother, welcome to Zimbabwe. Welcome to my home. I respect you for not giving up without trying. I don't know your story, but I know that it's traumatic enough to compel you to leave your home and friends, in pursuit of safety and greener pastures. Thank you for the gifts that you have brought to me and my family. I want you to feel at home, and to know that I care. *Mi casa, es tu casa.*"

If I knew what I know now, I would look in the eyes of a struggling student at Pote Secondary School and said, "Sister, I want you to pass your exams. I want you to understand the things that I teach. Please, tell me what I need to do to make things more intelligible for you."

If I had the heart that I have now, I would have held the hand of one of the so many orphans and abused children in the streets of Harare, and said, "Daughter, I know that you are a human being just like me. I know that life hasn't been fair to you. I respect you for keeping your head above the waters this far. Please, tell me your story."

A little kindness, encouragement, and love will make this world a better place to be. The right question to ask as I conclude my story is, "Have I achieved all that can be achieved in a lifetime?" The answer is yes and no. On the one hand, the answer is yes, for I have run a good race, and I have come this far. Considering where I started my journey, and where I am now, I have every reason to celebrate that which I have achieved. I have an education. I have a job. I have a family. I can't complain. I know of people who have tried very hard to change their lives but haven't succeeded. On the other hand, the answer is no. I still have dreams that haven't been realized. I would like to drive a bigger car, live in a mansion, and earn a fatter paycheck. I would like to donate money to those who are in need. In some secret place in my heart, I feel that the God who has brought me this far and has never failed to provide for my needs will always take me to a better place.

Made in the USA
San Bernardino, CA
23 February 2018